Martin Fitzgerald

The Pocket Essential

WOODY ALLEN

First published in Great Britain 2000 - this revised and updated edition published 2001 - by Pocket Essentials, 18 Coleswood Road, Harpenden, Herts, AL5 1EQ

Distributed in the USA by Trafalgar Square Publishing, PO Box 257, Howe Hill Road, North Pomfret, Vermont 05053

A CIP catalogue record for this book is available from the British Library.

ISBN 1-903047-05-6

2 4 6 8 10 9 7 5 3

Book typeset by Pdunk
Printed and bound by Cox & Wyman

for Claude and Josef

Acknowledgements

My thanks to Ellen Cheshire, John Ashbrook, Jane Sluijk-Brooks and Cinematheek Eindhoven for providing essential research materials, and to Nicole Thijs for providing the TV, video and laptop upon which to transform said materials into words. Most of all, thanks to Claude for taking a gamble on me, and to Josef for gambolling on me.

Note: This edition has been revised and updated to include *Sweet And Lowdown* and *Small Time Crooks*.

CONTENTS

Woody Allen: Dicing With Death

"Any man over 35 with whom death is not the main consideration is a fool."

It is easy to find out whether or not a joke is funny - you either laugh or you do not. It is an instantaneous reaction. But what happens in that instant? What idea or insight are you laughing at? Jokes can tell you a lot about the people telling them, as well as the people laughing at them. Jokes are like dreams, according to Freud, because they give expression to disagreeable elements that are usually prevented from entering consciousness. As a character says in *A Midsummer's Night Sex Comedy*, "No joke is completely untrue."

It is rare for a comedian to come through the 'funny' barrier, to be recognised for the insight and emotion contained within a joke. Consider, if you will, the jester in Shakespeare's *King Lear*, who tells the truth in the guise of jokes and witticisms.

Nobody takes comedians seriously. In the rare instance when a comedian takes a serious dramatic role they are often very good because their craft and timing is so finely honed it works as well for drama as it does for comedy. Think of Jerry Lewis in Martin Scorsese's *King Of Comedy*.

In a joke, the ideas are implicit rather than explicit. A joke must also seem spontaneous no matter how painstakingly laboured and crafted. So, in this series of contradictions, it must be assumed that comedy is actually drama dressed up. The comedian conceals how serious his thoughts are.

Comedy is not confrontational because it diffuses a situation, it releases tension. Drama, on the other hand, is confrontational, it focuses on problems, builds tension.

The joy of Woody Allen is that he is a comedian who reveals serious thoughts, he creates tension and makes us laugh at the same time.

Persona

A neurotic, fast-talking, therapy-seeking, New York-centric, Jewish male who has problems with women. Sound familiar? George in *Seinfeld*? Dr Joel Fleishman in *Northern Exposure*?

The Woody Allen persona is of a physical coward who lusts after women. He is good-hearted but clumsy, ineffectual and nervous - always stuttering and whining through the movie. On that rare occasion that the girl may be waiting behind the door for him, you know Allen cannot get in because the doorknob will come off in his hand.

Over the years, the persona has gradually changed. The Allen persona is now more likely to be in a domestic situation, or divorced with children. The persona has lived a life full of experiences, but still fears death and sexual impotence.

It must be stated that this persona is not the real Woody Allen. Yes, Woody Allen wears the same clothes in private life as he does when performing, but that does not mean that the persona and the person are one and the same. Just as the tramp is not Charlie Chaplin, and the elastic-faced lunatic is not Jerry Lewis, Woody Allen is no loser. He uses this persona to mask his personality and to mirror ours.

In fact, as if to make the point that the persona is not Woody Allen, his more recent movies have shown the young persona being performed by Kenneth Branagh in *Celebrity*, and John Cusack in *Bullets Over Broadway*.

I think it is also a mistake to think that we are supposed to feel empathy for this persona. Certainly, if you met such a person in real life you would either be sympathetic to his plight (the maternal instinct) or repulsed by his weakness (the survival of the fittest instinct) but you would not be able to stand his company for more than a couple of hours. The persona mirrors human weaknesses and frailties, and shows us what we are like inside.

Nobody likes to be reminded of their own faults, so to make the persona watchable/bearable Woody Allen the director has chosen to stand apart from his characters. Although one character may lead us through the story, there are many characters to deflect us away from the pain of that central character. Similarly, when a character is in pain, Allen's detached style allows us to watch and contemplate this pain in safety.

In his best roles, Allen makes the audience feel the absolute panic and terror he feels about his life - for example, losing the girl he loves, or not being able to write. This fear and desperation is repulsive to an audience, but somehow Allen's everyman appearance allows us to then empathise with him. He wins the audience back. It is interesting to note that those films where Allen appears, and does not play this kind of role well, often fail as a result.

Some film-makers want the audience to feel what the characters are feeling - for example, Alfred Hitchcock often showed a scene from a character's point of view - whereas others do not. Allen falls into the later category and I believe this detachment allows us to think more about the themes of the movies, and the relationships of many characters, rather than concentrating on just one character.

Although this detachment may sometimes seem cold and uninvolving, the simplicity and clarity in storytelling and theme is actually very difficult to achieve.

Career

Woody Allen is not dismissive of his early films - the ones with the jokes in them - but he does not consider them to be his best work. Although Allen began his career as a comedian (writing gags for TV, then doing stand-up routines), it is clear from his prose writing in *The New Yorker* that he aimed at something more significant. After his film-directing debut, he wrote a serious screenplay called *The Jazz Baby* but it was put aside in favour of *Bananas* (1971). He then had his first straight starring role in *The Front* (1976), and it was on the back of that that he emerged with his first serious film as a writer/director: *Annie Hall* (1977).

Woody Allen will tell you that it was by working with cinematographer Gordon Willis on *Annie Hall* that he became a mature film-maker. Willis was unlike other American cameramen - they used flat light to ensure everybody's face could be seen, whereas Willis used light and shade in an innovative way to tell the story. He was a great influence on American cameramen.

Allen discovered that if he went for funny lines, then people waited for the next joke rather than becoming interested in his characters. *Annie Hall* was the first of Allen's films to put his characters first, to tell the story, to be cinema rather than a critique of it (as in his earlier films), to let the jokes fit the characters rather than the other way around.

Annie Hall was both a commercial and artistic success. It won Oscars for Best Picture, Original Screenplay, Actress (Diane Keaton) and Director. Allen got three personal nominations for co-writing the screenplay, actor and director - a feat only previously matched by Orson Welles on *Citizen Kane*.

In fact, two thirds of Allen's films have been nominated for Oscars which is a staggering amount. Despite the kudos, Allen believes that rather than a 'best' or 'winner,' the Oscars should simply be a list of ten films they like.

Whatever the merits of the Oscars for *Annie Hall*, they gave Allen the mental and financial freedom to do *Interiors*, a sombre Chekhovian family drama filmed in a Bergmanesque style. It was not box-office dynamite, but it did serve to give notice that from now on, Woody Allen was a film-maker to be reckoned with.

Since then, Allen has consistently made a high-quality film almost every year.

Method

For many years Allen had a unique deal, secured for him by his agent Sam Cohen. Allen was given a budget each year and if he stayed under budget he had total freedom regarding script, actors, direction, editing, music and so on. If he went over budget, it came out of his pay.

Allen uses his freedom. He often rewrites on set and, after a first cut has been edited together, will reshoot up to 50% of each movie - actors even have the reshoots written into their contracts. The executives of the film company do not get to see a script or footage of the movie until Allen decides to show them the final cut ready for release.

A film begins with Allen thinking. He walks around his apartment, or around New York City, or around Central Park, and eats, and reads, and thinks. He finds an idea, develops it in his head and, when he has all the characters and the complete plot worked out, he sits down to write it. He writes rapidly. He does not mess about with synopses, and pitches and all that nonsense - he just writes the whole script. He then rewrites it once and does not look at it again until the day of shooting.

Having set up a deal where money is always available for him to film, pre-production begins the day after the script is finished and, once complete, filming will take anywhere from two to four months. Location filming is usually done first, followed by interiors on a sound stage - the interiors can take into account any necessary costume or continuity changes caused by the location work.

Whilst filming, Allen does not talk to many people. (One member of the crew worked for Allen for ten years and never talked to him.) Wearing a hat, often on his own, thoughtful, he is fully focused on the job at hand. He talks to the cameraman and actors when necessary, but there is not much chit-chat from him unless a personal friend visits the set.

Allen does not plan the shots in his movies. He okays the locations during pre-production then walks onto the set during filming, talks to the cameraman and discusses the set-up for a few minutes. The style of the movie is dictated by the style of the writing, because Allen considers himself a writer who directs rather than vice versa - and the precise application of that style depends on the location.

Once a set-up is decided, the cameraman gets the set lit using his electricians to place the lights on the stand-ins, and his grips to place the camera. This can take 30 minutes, or it can take up to two hours. The actors are brought on, told where to be in relation to the camera and they rehearse the camera movement. Then they roll the film and shoot it. Allen is looking for spontaneity, invention - nothing is writ in stone. He often asks actors to do it faster because scenes play slower on the screen.

Allen only supplies the main actors with full scripts - the rest just get their lines and nothing more, not even directions from him. The reason for this, Allen says, is so that actors do not invest their part with something that is not there, and he believes the actors then give a more natural reading of their own part - it also helps to maintain a certain secrecy about the film.

It takes about 15 minutes to do the takes, a few of which will be printed to give Allen options when editing. Sometimes it takes longer because of the wrong weather, lack of/too much light, costume changes, airplanes overhead, lunch breaks and union rules.

By not planning detailed shots ahead of time, Allen allows the writing of the project, and the locations, and the visual ideas of the cameraman, and the spontaneity of the actors, to gel together to create the style of the movie.

When filming is complete, editing for a month to six weeks follows, at the end of which a rough cut is ready. This is when Allen sees for the first time how the style has developed, and understands what he needs to reshoot to maintain a consistent style. Reshoots take three to four weeks to film. A final cut is ready a month after that.

For some of his movies around the late 1980s and early 1990s, his method evolved to a point where he did many master shots with no coverage (shots taken for safety reasons just in case the other shots do not edit together). One of his films was assembled by his editor Susan E Morse in one week because it consisted of only forty or so master shots.

When he has finished the final cut of one film, Woody Allen sits down to write the next. And so it goes. It is not uncommon for him to be filming a movie before the previous one is released. For example, when *Hannah And Her Sisters* was up for Oscars, *Radio Days* was premiering, the first version of *September* was being completed (it was reshot with a different cast), and *Another Woman* was written and scheduled for production.

Allen sees his films as part of a production line, each with its own ideas and genre and meaning. He does not think that his films should be hyped, that there should be any special tension because it has been three or five years since his last production. He wants to do one a year, every year, without high expectation and for them to be appreciated for their own merit. In this way he can feel free to write a light comedy, a sombre drama, a fantasy or a mystery without any undue pressure.

When he writes and directs films like *Interiors* or *September* or *Stardust Memories* or *Another Woman*, Allen knows they are not going to be blockbusters, and is more concerned about their artistic merit than with their commercial prospects. He makes them for his own enjoyment first, and hopes that the critics and the film company and the audience also like them.

When asked which he thinks are his best films, Allen invariably picks *The Purple Rose Of Cairo* simply because the finished film looked just like he had envisaged it in his head when he wrote it. It completely failed at the box office in America, but made money in Europe - a pattern which has repeated itself for virtually all of Allen's films since the late 1970s. Although few of his films are great commercial successes, they do make enough money to ensure that it is financially viable for the next one to be made.

Other films for which Allen had a positive feeling include *Husbands And Wives*, *Bullets Over Broadway* and *Stardust Memories*. Conversely, when he finished *Manhattan*, Allen was so disappointed with what he had done that he told the production company that he would do the next film for free if they did not release it. Luckily, the film company disagreed with Allen, and *Manhattan* went on to become a great success.

An illustration of Allen's low standing in household America (considering his high standing in film circles) is the way he is able to film for months on the streets of New York yet hardly attract more than a couple of ardent autograph hunters. One December day, whilst filming *Radio Days* mid-afternoon at Columbus Circle and Central Park West, the crowds were more interested in the second unit TV crew filming Stacy Keach as Mike Hammer getting out of a cab to buy a hot dog, than Woody Allen and his film crew setting up a period drama with people in costume. Go figure.

Collaborators

For more than 30 years, Allen has written and directed all his own films, and often acted in them. Quite rightly, this has thrust a great deal of attention onto Allen. However, you have got to remember that for most of this time, Allen has kept a close-knit film crew around him, whose recognition is long overdue. Three cinematographers (Gordon Willis (8 films), Sven Nykvist (4 films) and Carlo Di Palma (12 films)) and two editors (Ralph Rosenblum (5 films) and Ralph's former assistant Susan E Morse (20 films)) have maintained a visual continuity. For casting, he has relied on the advice of Juliet Taylor since time immemorial. Santo Loquasto has worked as either Costume or Production Designer for most films from *Stardust Memories* to the present. Jeffrey Kurland has been with the crew since *Broadway Danny Rose*, and has even been on screen (he was the unseen documentary interviewer in *Husbands And Wives*). The list goes on and on, from key grips, camera operators, prop men and make-up to bit actors.

Allen's once-a-year turnover not only allows him to explore a variety of ideas and subjects, it also keeps his crew employed. They do not work for enormous sums of money (the big name actors know that they will probably only get union rates for the job, but they accept that because it is *Woody Allen*), but at least they have a regular job. In 1998, cutbacks had to be made, and many of his long-timers left. He and Sweetland Films subsequently ended their seven-picture relationship with *Small Time Crooks*, and Allen has signed a three-picture deal with Steven Spielberg's DreamWorks SKG. The 65-year-old Allen is still going strong.

Themes

Allen has compared his films to novels. There are several reasons for this comparison. First of all, many of his films are about writers and the creative process (a subject novelists often write about). Secondly, Allen usually has one of the characters tell the story - film in the first person. Furthermore, by seeing the narrator's thoughts, we do not necessarily see events in chronological order, or accurately. For example, both *Annie Hall* and *Stardust Memories* are the remembrances of the central character, a discussion inside their heads which we are watching unfold.

Allen also thinks of himself as a writer who happens to direct films of his work, so that the style of the film is wholly dependent on the style and subject of the written word. This means that each new project often brings with it a new way of making movies, new problems, new solutions. He even takes the analogy further and considers his reshoots to be the equivalent to rewrites of novels.

Such is Allen's commitment to writing that he has said that if he were unable to find the money to make films, he would not be too bothered, and would write plays. Failing that, he would write novels. He has enough money not to worry about his personal circumstances, and says that he writes for the pleasure of it, not the profit.

Films are pieces of time and, like a writer, Allen likes to play around with it, to jump through time, elongate it, condense it. If a writer can span a generation with a sentence, then why can't a film-maker do the same thing? Allen is not afraid to try. He keeps it light, seemingly unstructured, to follow the story rather than sticking to any one rigid filming style. In the same way that jokes can cover a lot of hard work, Allen's seemingly effortless direction is also very difficult.

Another important point to remember is that Allen is associating himself with literary rather than commercial novels - this means that at the resolution of the story the central character has learned from their experience and has changed. A commercial film often means that the status quo has been maintained rather than upset.

In the earlier 'funny' films, there were often references to, and jokes about, other well-known films. Then Allen started to play with how the story is told, making explicit the fact that his films are stories not reality. So, for example, in *Annie Hall*, during an argument with a man in a cinema queue, Allen says that the man misquoted Marshall McLuhan, and then produces McLuhan to verify the misquoting, hence winning the argument. To camera, Allen makes a comment to the effect that he wishes this could happen in real life.

The creative process later became the theme for *Deconstructing Harry*, about writer Harry Block, who uses the lives of the people nearest him as the basis for his work (just as Holly in *Hannah And Her Sisters* uses her family as raw material for her writing). It features a hilarious cameo by Robin Williams as an actor who is going out of focus and so cannot be filmed - his family even have to wear glasses to bear looking at him. As well as a metaphor for Harry Block not being focused on his work, it also works on another level - here we have Robin Williams in a cameo appearance in a movie, for which many film companies would gladly pay millions of dollars, yet Allen has probably got him for union minimum wages and we do not even get to see him!

Although much of Allen's work in the 1960s and early 1970s is politically aware and has many political references - Fielding Mellish bound and gagged whilst on trial in *Bananas* echoes Bobby Searle bound and gagged at the trial of the Chicago Seven - this had all but disappeared by the late 1970s. Allen sometimes comments on how society interacts (most notably *Zelig*) but mostly he uses personal relationships as his subject matter. And, further, he often analyses what is going on inside one or two people, to show contrast. In *Celebrity*, for example, Kenneth Branagh dreams of becoming a writer but he will never achieve that fame, whilst Judy Davis has fame and success thrust upon her.

From the very beginning, Allen has asked the big questions about life and death (*Interiors*, *Crimes And Misdemeanors*), about happiness and despair (*Stardust Memories*, *Celebrity*), about finding and losing love (*Annie Hall*, *Manhattan*). Often, at the end of the movie, it is the male characters who are weakened and in despair, and the female characters who are strong, resolute and emboldened by the experience.

Since *Annie Hall*, Allen has found it much easier to write female characters, and many of them are stronger than his male characters. "For some reason," Allen explained, "I started to write basically from the woman's point of view all the time... I don't know how it happened or why or when, but something turned around." Many actresses owe a lot to this sudden change, including Dianne Wiest, who won an Oscar for her role in *Hannah And Her Sisters* and again for 1994's *Bullets Over Broadway*.

Almost single-handedly, Allen has created more meaningful roles for women than most of his American peers put together. Who can forget the female-dominated families in *Interiors* or *Hannah And Her Sisters*? One of the reasons he attributes to this is that it is easy to find strong women actors in America, but very difficult to find male actors who can play characters who display a full range of emotions. Most American actors play virile parts - they do not cry, or show any kind of weakness. This is why Allen has used many English actors - because they are happy to play normal, regular, vulnerable characters.

By way of contrast, you may notice a lack of ethnic groups as characters in Allen's movies. This is surprising considering most of his films are set in New York, but Allen explains that first of all he does not know the black and Hispanic cultures well enough to write about them and also blacks do not live in the areas of New York he writes about. Allen gets flak from pressure groups for not including more ethnic races, and also from Jewish groups saying he is too critical of Jewish culture. Allen has said he writes for the authenticity of the scene, not to fill some quota.

Allen is a middle-class film-maker. The middle class often come under attack from the artistic community. Tolstoy said that the middle class keep society functioning, and that is certainly Allen's point of view. Allen shows families who function despite the problems they may have. They keep themselves busy, fill their lives with as many distractions as possible, so that they do not have to think about the big things in life. Isaac comments on this in *Manhattan*, as does Steffi in *September*, and Mickey in *Hannah And Her Sisters*.

One of the best characters in Woody Allen's films (and certainly the most used) is Manhattan. It is not just the location, which can hide every type of human existence in its nooks and crannies, but the noise and atmosphere. The noise is usually the sound of people talking - city life is about verbal communication. As Allen pointed out, if a film is about country life then it is about ritual and labour since that is how people communicate on a day-to-day basis, but city life is about chatting, gossiping, arguing, whispering, discussing, eulogising, pontificating. This is why, in Allen's films, you will often see two characters walking down the street, discussing their problems, oblivious of the life teeming around them.

Endgame

Watching all Allen's films in close succession is an education. Suddenly, you realise why he has such affection for Dostoyevsky, Bergman, Kurosawa and other 20th-Century heavyweights - they all talk about death. But that is not the whole story, because he enjoys the spontaneous quality of jazz, the romanticism of Cole Porter, and the laughter of the Marx Brothers. Death is inevitable. Love is unpredictable. Enjoy life while you can.

In Bergman's *The Seventh Seal*, we see Death playing chess. Life is a game. Sometimes you win, sometimes you lose, but you are most alive when you are playing. Chess is too highbrow for Woody Allen. He prefers to play dice with death, and it looks as though he is thoroughly enjoying himself.

Beau Jest

Allan Stewart Konigsberg was born in Brooklyn on December 1 1935, within walking distance of 25 cinemas. At the age of three, Allan saw his first movie, *Snow White And The Seven Dwarfs*. He was so entranced by it that he ran up to touch the screen. He became a regular movie-goer at the age of five. During summer, he went every day if he had the money. During winter, he went Saturday and Sunday for sure, and sometimes Friday evening. He ingested everything: romantic comedies by Preston Sturges; slapstick comedies by the Marx Brothers and Charlie Chaplin; murder mysteries starring Humphrey Bogart and James Cagney, etc.

Whilst inhabiting the local movie theatres, Allan was deeply affected by the contrast between the harshness of reality he saw on the streets of Brooklyn, and the fantasy he saw portrayed in the cinema - big white houses, white dresses, smart talk, everything turns okay in the end. In his own movies, Allen writes about his own fantasy world, and shows us the tension between fantasy and reality. Alvy Singer's fantasy is to be with Annie Hall but he cannot, so he writes a play where they are together. In *The Purple Rose Of Cairo*, Mia Farrow would very much like her screen fantasy man Jeff Daniels to be real - he becomes real and she finds that it is impossible to live with her fantasy.

Allan's experience with poverty was very real - his parents argued all the time over money. He also had his first brush with death. At the age of three he was in his crib when a nanny held him tightly in a bundle so that he could not breathe. She told Allan that she could smother him and throw him in the garbage and no one would know. Since that time, he has been afraid of small spaces - he will not ride elevators or go through long tunnels.

Despite Allan's spindly appearance, and his preoccupation with films, it is surprising to find out that he was quite a good athlete as a boy. There is little proof of his sporting prowess in his films - although *Annie Hall* features some tennis - but he is an active spectator of baseball, basketball, boxing, football, tennis and golf, either in person or via television.

In his early teens, Allan listened to Sidney Bechet on record and was instantly converted into a jazz baby, picking up the records of Bunk Johnson, Jelly Roll Morton and others. He learnt soprano saxophone then clarinet. Some years later, whilst doing cabaret in San Francisco, Allen was listening in to Turk Murphy, who persuaded/forced Allen to play. From then on Allen could not be stopped. He formed his own band, The New Orleans Funeral And Ragtime Orchestra, who played at Michael's Pub in New York City on Monday nights from 1971 until it closed in 1997. Allen now plays with the Eddie Davis New Orleans Jazz Band at the Café Carlyle every Monday night. A documentary film of their exploits on tour, called *Wild Man Blues* was released in 1998.

In the 1950s, the movie art houses began to show Ingmar Bergman's films - *Summer With Monika*, *The Naked Night*, *Wild Strawberries*, *The Seventh Seal* etc. - and Bergman became a lifelong favourite, although the original reason Allan and Mickey Rose went to see *Summer With Monika* was because they heard there was nudity in it. There were also other film-makers to admire: Frederico Fellini, Vittorio De Sica, Michelangelo Antonioni, René Clair, Jean Renoir and the rest.

As well as sports, jazz and the movies, Allan's other passion was magic. As a kid he got a magic kit, and he used to practise for hours to perfect his sleight of hand technique. One day he was in a magic shop when Milton Berle walked in. They began talking and Allan auditioned there and then for a guest spot as a magic act - his hands fluffed the audition and a promising magic act was cut off in its prime. Berle later appeared in *Broadway Danny Rose*.

The magic act got Allan onto the stage - at Weinstein's Majestic Bungalow Colony. This was a resort in the Catskill Mountains, which is also featured in the scene in *Broadway Danny Rose* where Danny is trying to persuade Phil Clomsky to book one of his acts (a blind xylophone player, a one-legged tap dancer and a one-armed juggler).

At school, although he rarely attended and got bad grades, Allan was a popular guy, always ready with a joke or quip. Aged 15, he began sending jokes into paper columnists under the name Woody Allen, and was regularly featured by name, although he got no money for his work. Then a press agent employed Allen to come into Manhattan after school for three hours a day to write jokes - Allen got $20 a week.

Allen's parents did not consider the joke-writing to be a career, and asked when he was going to get a 'proper' job. To fulfil their expectations, he enrolled in the Motion Picture Production class at New York University. Allen liked watching the movies, but he hated the discussions and analysis afterwards, so he attended the films (often in movie theatres around Times Square) and not the classes - he was thrown off the course.

Another passion was women - a passion he shared with all his friends. Although they found him funny, women had a hard time visualising him as a love interest. The reason, Allen soon realised, was that the particular type of women he liked - thin, long black hair, black dresses - were invariably the beatnik/art student type who preferred hanging out in Greenwich Village, talking about Sartre, Kerouac and the meaning of life, than hanging out with funny, uneducated Allen. To get to talk to them, Allen decided to educate himself. He began reading books, starting with the American classics of Ernest Hemingway, John Steinbeck and William Faulkner. He soon moved onto the French existentialists and then the Russians - Fyodor Dostoyevsky and Leo Tolstoy - and so began his self-education of the world of books, art, plays and films. As a result of this life experience, Allen sometimes portrays the central character in his films trying to chat up women by making references to poets, artists and philosophy.

Allen was trying to develop his own personality as a performer, and friends encouraged him to appear on stage. He used a friend's material, which Allen thought very professional, and was a success. He then appeared in Summer Theatre, writing and performing sketches. This was seen by Sid Caesar's stand-in, and Allen was hired to write for Sid Caesar's TV show. Allen was one of Caesar's stable of comic writers which included Mel Brooks, Carl Reiner and Neil Simon. Working with Larry Gelbert, who later adapted *M.A.S.H.* for television, Allen earned an Emmy nomination.

In later years, Allen would dismiss writing for television as a worthless exercise because the work was not appreciated while it was being broadcast, and when it was finished it just disappeared into the ether forever. He once said that some of the great TV writers were like Renaissance painters working on sand.

While working in a small place as a comedian, and doubling up as a musician in the band, Allen met Harlene Rosen. They became friends and married in March, 1956 - she was 17, he was 20. As Allen became more of a comedy writer for hire, the money started to roll in, bringing his earnings up to $1,700 a week. Then he threw that all away in 1960 to become a stand-up comic.

This decision was made for the simple reason that Allen had written so many jokes and sketches for other people, in their style, that he wanted to write something for himself, in his own style. His new managers, Jack Rollins and Charles H Joffe, took Allen on as a writer, but they loved his performances when he read his work to them and told Allen he should go on stage. They pushed him to go on stage at *The Blue Angel* in New York. Allen only got the gig because of Rollins' reputation - Rollins had been responsible for introducing and grooming Harry Belafonte, Mike Nichols and Elaine May among many others. From there Allen went on to *The Duplex* before making a name for himself at *The Bitter End* in Greenwich Village. Rollins and Joffe came to each of Allen's performances to discuss the script and his routines. It took two years for the terrified Allen to become comfortable with being on stage, getting his delivery right and working up his material for a paying audience.

Rollins and Joffe became Allen's managers on a handshake and, from that day until this, no legal documentation has passed between them, even though they have negotiated deals for Allen worth millions of dollars. In more recent years, they have managed Robin Williams, David Letterman and Billy Crystal.

Joffe once made the comment that ironically, a good manager teaches his ward to become independent, and not need a manager. This truth was learnt the hard way by Rollins - after he got Belafonte started, Belafonte left for a better-known manager. If this sounds like the germ of an idea for a movie named *Broadway Danny Rose*, then I suspect you may be right.

As a stand-up comedian, Allen took his cue from Mort Sahl. Sahl worked the cabaret circuit where normally the comedians wore tuxedos, talked with false sincerity and joked about President Eisenhower and golf. Sahl had none of that. He walked on in slacks and jumper, a *New York Times* under one arm, sat down and talked about relationships, politics and popular culture. He made his digressions and stream of consciousness comments seem natural and unforced, while in fact they were scripted and planned. After seeing Sahl, Allen, who had only been a writer up until then, decided he wanted to perform as well.

Harlene thought that Allen was wasting his talent becoming a cheap comic when he could not only become a great comic writer but a great writer full stop. The strain of two years of stand-up, plus their growing apart resulted in Allen moving out in 1961, and divorce in 1962.

Through his TV connections, Allen got the opportunity to write a pilot for a new TV series called *The Laughmaker*. Filmed in 1962, this half-hour show starred Louise Lasser, Alan Alda and Paul Hampton, but it failed to inspire ABC and a series was never made. Allen later married Louise Lasser, in 1966, and they divorced in 1969.

Allen was performing in cabaret when film producer Charles K Feldman took a liking to his work and hired him to write the script for *What's New, Pussycat?* (1965). This was originally a vehicle for Warren Beatty - in fact, the title was his salutation when picking up the telephone and talking to women. Director Clive Donner did not really know what to do with the script, or how to direct it. Another problem was that Allen had too many of the best lines, so some of his scenes were rewritten for Peter O'Toole and Peter Sellers. The O'Toole character is what Allen aspires to, and Sellers' character is the beast he fears he may become. However, Allen's character is not the centre of attention, (Romy Schneider, Capucine, Paula Prentiss, Ursula Andress, Richard Burton and Louise Lasser also helped to divert it) so a lot of the subtext is lost and only the funny lines remain. Allen did not like the film and vowed to direct his own scripts in the future.

After the runaway success of *What's New, Pussycat?*, the producers wanted to repeat that and so the rights to Ian Fleming's first Bond book, *Casino Royale*, were acquired, and many of the same people from *What's New, Pussycat?* were hired: Woody Allen, Peter Sellers, Ursula Andress, Burt Bacharach (songs), and Richard Williams (animated titles). To give you some idea of the chaos involved in the making of the film (four or more directors worked on it), Allen was paid a lot of money to appear but had to stay in London at the producer's expense for six months before he was called in for filming. At is happens, Allen only appeared in two scenes, the first and last, as the villain Jimmy Bond.

It is rarely acknowledged that Woody Allen has written anything other than films. Allen made good use of his six months in London by writing a play called *Don't Drink The Water* (1966). A Broadway hit, it is about the Hollanders, an American family holidaying in Europe, who are pursued after taking illegal pictures of military places. They take refuge in the American Embassy, where Father Drobney, a priest who does magic tricks, is also seeking sanctuary. The Hollanders are helped/hindered by the incompetent Ambassador's son, Axel Magee, who is too honest for his own good. In the end, the Hollanders and Father Drobney are smuggled out, and Susan Hollander and Axel marry. The play was filmed in 1969, directed by Howard Morris and starring Jackie Gleason as Walter Hollander. In 1994, Allen directed and starred in a TV version with Michael J Fox.

Play It Again, Sam (1969), another Broadway hit, follows the trials and tribulations of Allan Felix, a film critic who needs to revive his sex life and self-respect after his wife leaves him. Friends Dick and Linda Christie try to arrange various liaisons for Allan, and he even consults the spirit of Humphrey Bogart for advice. Allan and Linda fall in love, become intimate, and then Allan has to give her up à la *Casablanca*.

Felix is Allen's first and only role in a play. Allen thought it the easiest job in the world. He did what he wanted all day - perhaps write, perhaps relax with a book - then walked over to the theatre for 8pm, went on stage, the curtain went up, he played with his friends for an hour and a half, the curtain came down, and two hours later he was in a restaurant.

When the Broadway show was running, the film rights to *Play It Again, Sam* were sold. Allen did not want to direct because it was now in the past for him. He quotes Tennessee Williams who said that when a writer finishes a work, he transcends it. (This also applies to his films - Allen refuses to watch any of them once released.) Other actors were offered the part of Felix but they turned it down. However, four years later, when Allen was better known, he was offered the part and accepted it, as did the rest of the original Broadway cast. *Play It Again, Sam* (1972) was ably directed by Herbert Ross.

Allen also wrote some one-act plays which have rarely, if ever, been performed. *Death Knocks* is about 57-year-old dress manufacturer Nat Ackerman who plays gin rummy with Death. This is obviously a take on the game of chess Death usually plays with his victims. Ackerman wins. Death does not have enough money for the fare home, so he hangs around until the following evening to recoup his losses. Ackerman is so simple-minded that he does not have the sense to fear Death.

Death is about Kleinman (means 'little man' in Yiddish) who is forced to join a vigilante hunt for a murderer. He tries to find safety and, at the same time find out what his role in the hunt is. He is accused of being the murderer, but news arrives just in time saying that the killer has been caught elsewhere. Kleinman then meets the murderer: Death. He is fatally stabbed by Death and the vigilantes continue their hunt for the murderer. This was the basis for Allen's film *Shadows And Fog*.

God is set in 500BC. Two Greeks in an empty amphitheatre, writer and actor, Hepatitis and Diabetes, are trying to find an ending to their play *The Slave*, in which they both have roles. Questions are asked about the nature of God. Does He exist? Did we invent Him because we need rules to live by? Freedom of choice or pre-ordination? People in the audience rise, argue, join the cast on stage or leave the theatre. In their own way, all the characters become free, but they want their lives to be scripted by God. We are made aware that Allen is the creator of the play, their God. It ends with the two Greeks still trying to find an ending to the play.

The Query begins with Abraham Lincoln asking his press secretary to plant a question at his next press conference. The question is: How long do you think a man's leg should be? Lincoln's answer: Long enough to reach the ground. The question was originally asked by a farmer Will Haines, who presented the riddle rather than ask for a pardon for his son who had been sentenced to death for falling asleep whilst on guard duty. Lincoln is going to pardon the son at the upcoming press conference. The play is a metaphor for the way comedy can help people to discover inner truth and emotion - the story of Allen's creative life!

A later play, *The Floating Light Bulb* (1982), is about the illusions we have in daily life which prevent us from altering our reality. Set in 1945, it is about the Pollack family - father Max, mother Enid and son Paul. Max is a waiter who resents Enid's artificial airs and wants to run away to Florida or Nevada with his mistress Betty. (Betty dreams of being a fashion designer.) Enid is an alcoholic who dreams of having an affair with Jerry Wexler. (Jerry is a third-rate agent who dreams of having that one great act, but he is so bad he would not be able to pick up Danny Rose's cast-offs.) Paul constantly practises his magic act, encouraged by his mother, but he is completely useless.

Allen also wrote prose for the very prestigious magazine *The New Yorker* - they published the first thing he sent, so he sent them more, many more. Many of his pieces from *The New Republic*, *Esquire*, *Playboy* and *The New Yorker* are collected in his best-selling books *Getting Even* (1971), *Without Feathers* (1975), *Side Effects* (1980) and *The Illustrated Woody Allen Reader* (1993).

What's Up Tiger Lily? (1966)

Producer & Director Woody Allen, Writers Woody Allen & Julie Bennett & Frank Buxton & Louise Lasser & Len Maxwell & Mickey Rose & Bryan Wilson & Kazuo Yamada

Cast: Woody Allen (Narrator/Host/Voice), Eisei Amamoto (Bartender with Peter Lorre accent), Steven Boone, Joe Butler, Mie Hama (Teri Yaki), Susumu Kurobe (Wing Fat), Tatsuya Mihashi (Phil Moscowitz), Tadao Nakamaru (Shepherd Wong), John Sebastian (as The Lovin' Spoonful), Akiko Wakabayashi (Suki Yaki), 80 mins

Background: Allen took an existing Japanese movie *Key Of Keys* (1964, dir Senkichi Taniguchi), which was a spoof of the James Bond movies, cut it up, rearranged the scenes, filmed some new ironic sequences and redubbed the whole thing with his friends. Allen's story is about Phil Moscowitz, a loveable Jewish rogue, whose mission is to find the stolen recipe for the world's best egg salad. The dialogue was ad libbed by the actors.

Allen appears four times: a cartoon in the opening credits; telling us how he made the film; as one half of a couple having a secret tryst in the projection booth whose shadows are projected onto the screen; and on a sofa eating an apple ignoring China Lee's striptease on the other half of the split-screen.

This film is playing with the form and expectations of movies. A movie is not a real thing - it is people pretending to be something else, but people believe it to be real. Allen stretches this suspension of belief to its limit. How can the Japanese actor be Jewish? Why would anybody go to all this trouble for an egg salad recipe? Allen appears at the beginning to tell us this is a movie. When we see the characters in the projection booth, it re-enforces the fact that we are watching a movie. There is even a sequence where a hair gets caught in the film and a hand takes away the hair.

Allen describes this as a dreadful experience for him and says he tried to sue the producer before it was released. However, when it came out to good reviews, Allen dropped the suit because he did not think it worth the effort. He considers the film sleep-inducing.

23

Jest A Moment

Having written the very successful *What's New, Pussycat?*, Allen wrote a new script with his childhood friend Mickey Rose. Allen gave the completed screenplay to Val Guest, who had just directed him in *Casino Royale* (1967). Val loved it, but his production company did not. Allen offered it to Jerry Lewis - it was the same story there as well. Salvation came in the form of Palomar Pictures, a new production company that needed talent. The budget for the screenplay was less than one million dollars, and it was by the writer of the enormously successful *What's New, Pussycat?*, so they figured they could take a chance. Allen was given carte blanche, final cut, no interference and had no problems with the production company.

Take The Money And Run (1969)

Director Woody Allen, Writers Woody Allen & Mickey Rose

Cast: Woody Allen (Virgil Starkwell), Janet Margolin (Louise), Marcel Hillaire (Fritz), Jackson Beck (The Narrator), Henry Leff (Father Starkwell), Ethel Sokolow (Mother Starkwell), Louise Lasser (Kay Lewis), Dan Frazer (The Psychiatrist), 85 mins

"The prisoners were fed one hot meal per day: a bowl of steam."

Story: Virgil Starkwell is an incompetent criminal whose only claim to fame is that a film crew is following him around. This is a skit on the then-hip style of cinéma vérité - a hand-held camera, interviews to camera, natural sound and a general acknowledgement of the camera's existence. Having established the style, Allen then destroys it. He assembled footage of an old baseball game, newly filmed footage of Virgil and his grandfather playing catch, and found footage of Kaiser Wilhelm, then put on a voice-over to give it a totally different meaning - in a similar fashion to the totally fictitious *What's Up, Tiger Lily?* There is footage of Virgil as a boy which could not exist. Then, when Virgil and Louise are on their honeymoon, we see them making love - surely they would not do this with a camera crew in the same room? Allen is showing that cinéma vérité is a style, and that there is no truth in vérité at all.

Background: Before filming began, Allen was slightly apprehensive about directing and wanted to find out how to do it. He met with director Arthur Penn (*Bonnie And Clyde* (1967)), who talked about colour matching and other important practical matters. As regards directing, Penn thought it straightforward.

Allen's first important decisions were to select the costume designer, cameraman and art director, but ended up firing both the costume designer and cameraman after a few days. Allen had rather grandiose ideas about who he wanted for cameraman. Kurosawa's perhaps? He telegrammed Michelangelo Antonioni's cameraman Carlo Di Palma, who was unable to come. Di Palma kept the telegram, and would first work for Allen on *Hannah And Her Sisters* in 1985.

The first day's shooting was in San Quentin prison and Allen was so excited he cut his nose shaving, which you can see in the final film. Playing it safe, he took shots from many different angles, took many takes of each angle, and had them all printed. This would give him the coverage he needed to edit the film together. Allen's working method continued like this for four or five films until he gained the confidence to do longer takes, with less angles and less prints.

When filming ended, Allen got into the editing suite and discovered that scenes he had thought funny on the set were not funny on film. So he started editing everything out until he had nothing left. The producers brought in Ralph Rosenblum, who told Allen all the jokes were great, and asked why he was cutting them all out? It was the start of an editing relationship which would last until *Interiors*. One of the editing tricks Rosenblum showed Allen was to put a music track in the background - whether or not that track is going to be used in the final film - and then edit the film to the rhythm of the music. It is something Allen does to this day, which is why so many of his films feature music from records rather than music written for the film. Allen also likes to use the natural sound of the actors and their surroundings during the take, rather than dubbing their voices in later - it sounds better and saves time & money.

Subtext: This is a film about film. References: *West Side Story* (1961) the gang open their switchblades and Virgil's blade flies off; *Bonnie & Clyde* (1967) Virgil shows his gun to a cashier through his trouser fly, so the gun is a phallus; *The Hustler* (1961) Virgil's career as a pool shark; *The Seven Year Itch* (1955) Virgil takes his suit from the fridge and shoes from the freezer à la Marilyn Monroe; *I Am A Fugitive From A Chain Gang* (1932) Virgil in a chain gang; *Cool Hand Luke* (1967) a sadistic warden puts Virgil in the cooler with an insurance agent; *Monkey Business* (1931) Virgil talks like Groucho Marx, and also Virgil's parents wear Groucho masks when interviewed.

The whole film recreates the story of the first film in this genre, Fritz Lang's *You Only Live Once* (1937). As homage, when Virgil ironically plans to rob a bank with a film crew as cover, the director is called Fritz - they even rehearse their lines. But when they get there, they find another gang also robbing the bank. Of course, we are watching a documentary film crew, filming the film crew, filming the robbery.

Allen further comments on the visual within the film: Virgil's glasses are broken several times throughout the movie; the cashiers cannot read Virgil's stick-up note; Virgil's glasses pass from him to Louise whilst they are making love; and when attacked, Virgil puts his hands to his eyes.

One of Allen's recurring themes is psychoanalysis. Here, a psychoanalyst is asked his opinion about Virgil's actions.

The Verdict: This is great fun, and it still has a certain freshness to it. It is interesting to note that Allen went on to make other documentary-type movies - *Zelig* and *Husbands And Wives*. 4/5

Bananas (1971)

Director Woody Allen, Writers Woody Allen & Mickey Rose

Cast: Woody Allen (Fielding Mellish), Louise Lasser (Nancy), Carlos Montalbán (General Emilio M Vargas), Natividad Abascal (Yolanda), Howard Cosell, Roger Grimsby, Don Dunphy, Allen Garfield (Man On Cross), Danny DeVito (Man Sitting In Honeymoon Suite), Sylvester Stallone (Subway Tough), 82 mins

Working Title: El Weirdo

Story: Fielding Mellish, a products tester, falls for Nancy, a CCNY student activist petitioning against the Latin American dictatorship in San Marcos. When Nancy breaks off their romance, Mellish goes after her, becomes part of the revolution in San Marcos and ends up as President. Returning to America, he asks for foreign aid, but is arrested and charged with treason. A trial ensues.

Subtext: At this stage in his career, Allen liked to have a thin story upon which to hang the comedy sequences. He concentrated on making it funny and face-paced, but there are still themes inherent in all his work. Here, as usual, the Allen persona is an outsider. This is shown literally when a doorknob comes off when he is about to ask a secretary for a date - he is not allowed through the door. When Nancy comes to visit there are many locks on his door, which suggests he is keeping himself apart from the world. And when he is trying to impress Nancy in one scene, he leans against a door - he is trying to get in. Eventually, when he becomes President of San Marcos, he is as inside as anybody can get, so he tells the citizens to wear their underwear on the outside and makes Swedish the new official language - thus making everybody an outsider in their own country.

This is also a story about exploitation. When Fielding first appears he is wearing a red, white and blue shirt - he is an American everyman character. But by the end of the movie he has been manipulated and used by politicians (America & San Marcos), religious groups (Jewish), popular culture (TV) and women (Nancy).

Again, Allen plays with film conventions. When Fielding receives a dinner invite, we hear dreamy music - Fielding opens a cupboard and finds a harpist inside it playing the music we are hearing. Later, when Fielding and Nancy are breaking up, we see blurry photography and lyrical music which is the film convention for lovers coming together. Probably the best satirical element is the use of *Howard Cosell's Wide World Of Sport* - a real TV sports program - which advertises the upcoming assassination of the President of San Marcos, and when the President is shot dead Cosell then proceeds to attempt an interview with him. Later, Cosell also features the Mellishes' wedding night on his program. There are a few film homages in there including the tumbling baby carriage from Sergei Eisenstein's *Battleship Potemkin*, and runaway gadgetry reminiscent of Chaplin's *Modern Times*.

Background: As a debut film, *Take The Money And Run* was successful enough for Allen to sign a contract with United Artists. They gave him free reign, and Allen wrote a period jazz story called *The Jazz Baby*. It was a serious script and the United Artists executives were alarmed - it was definitely not what they expected from funny man Allen. Allen did not want to force them to make a film they did not want, so he wrote *Bananas* for them instead. *The Jazz Baby* was later filmed as *Sweet And Lowdown*.

Look out for Sylvester Stallone in his film debut, as one of the thugs on the subway. In some towns the film is advertised as *Bananas*, starring Woody Allen and Sylvester Stallone. If you think that is a weird pairing then remember that they appeared together as voice-overs to the feature-length cartoon *Antz* (1999).

The Verdict: Amusing in parts but it does not linger in the mind. 3/5

Allen was not only writing for film, he was also continuing a career in television. He had TV specials in 1968 (with Billy Graham and Candice Bergman), and in 1970 (with Liza Minnelli) which were not commercial successes, but the final nail in the coffin came in 1971 with *The Politics Of Woody Allen: Men of Crisis - The Harvey Wallinger Story*. Allen wrote, directed and starred in this 25-minute fictionalised documentary for PBS, in which he played Harvey Wallinger, a swipe at Henry Kissinger. At the time, the Nixon administration was putting pressure on PBS by cutting back on their money and issuing all sorts of threats, so PBS wanted to make a few cuts to the show. Allen refused to cave and the show was not aired. Although he admitted the show was in bad taste, he went on to comment that it was, "hard to do anything about the administration that wouldn't be in bad taste." Allen assures us we are not missing a masterpiece, but if you are desperate, New York's Museum of Radio and Television has a copy.

Everything You Always Wanted To Know About Sex (But Were Afraid To Ask) (1972)

Director & Writer Woody Allen, Book David Reuben

Cast: Woody Allen (Victor/Fabrizio/The Fool/Sperm), John Carradine (Doctor Bernardo), Lou Jacobi (Sam), Louise Lasser (Gina), Anthony Quayle (The King), Tony Randall (The Operator), Lynn Redgrave (The Queen), Burt Reynolds (Switchboard), Gene Wilder (Dr Doug Ross), Sidney Miller (George), Regis Philbin, Alan Caillou (The Fool's Father), 87 mins

Story 1: Do Aphrodisiacs Work? Felix the Court Jester fails to amuse the King and lusts after the Queen. While the King is away, the ghost of his father orders him to bed the Queen, but Felix cannot get at the Queen due to the obstruction of a chastity belt. Felix is discovered and beheaded. The obvious film reference is *A Man For All Seasons* (1966), with bits of Shakespeare's *Hamlet* and *Macbeth* thrown in for good measure. Felix was Allen's name in *Play It Again, Sam* - a man who seduced his best friend's wife.

Story 2: What Is Sodomy? Doug Ross, a Jackson Heights general practitioner, is happily married and affluent. Then Milos, an Armenian shepherd, asks for help - he is in love with a sheep named Daisy but she rejects him. Dr Ross meets the sheep and falls in love with her. A passionate affair ensues, a hotel tryst, a suspicious wife and discovery. Their love can overcome any social or specie differences, thinks Ross. He loses his home, they move to worse and worse accommodation, until Ross ends up on the streets - Daisy leaves him. The breakfast sequence with the lengthening dinner table is a reference to Orson Welles' *Citizen Kane* (1941).

Story 3: Why Do Some Women Have Trouble Reaching An Orgasm? Fabrizio and Gina, Italian newly-weds have sex problems - Gina cannot reach orgasm - until they discover that Gina can only achieve orgasm when she has sex in public places. They have a lot of sex… A parody on the art house film in general and Italian cinema (especially Michelangelo Antonioni) in particular, it features some decidedly unartistic subtitles. For example, whilst making love, Gina exclaims, "Go easy on my hymen." The bad translation echoes the couple's problem - a lack of communication. Allen is playing against type here - he plays a sexual athlete called Fabrizio, meaning 'maker,' who cannot satisfy his wife.

Story 4: Are Transvestites Homosexuals? We see Sam and Tess, a middle-aged couple dressing to go to their daughter's fiancé's parents for dinner. Over dinner Sam, a coarse man, feels inferior to the successful host. Sam goes upstairs, dresses in his hostess' clothes and, when surprised, hides on the balcony, has his purse stolen and in the ensuing chaos his secret is revealed. As they undress for bed, Tess talks to her husband in soft tones but this voice 'dresses' her true feeling of revulsion. Sam is a sad character and we feel for him because he is trying to show something gentle inside his coarse exterior. Perhaps Allen's first successful marriage of comedy and tragedy on film.

Story 5: What Are Sex Perverts? A TV game show with four contestants trying to guess who is the most perverted guest. The Rabbi is the winner - he likes to be whipped by his mistress as his wife eats pork. Includes advertisements.

Story 6: Are The Findings Of Doctors And Clinics Who Do Sexual Research Accurate? Sexuality researcher Victor Shakopopolous meets Sunday supplement reporter Helen and he takes her to interview Dr Bernardo. The bad Doctor plans to use them in an experiment. They escape, the lab explodes and a forty-foot-high breast escapes and terrorises the countryside. "They usually travel in pairs," warns the Sheriff. Victor lures the breast into a bra and order is restored. It starts as a parody of the gothic horror/mad scientist movie and then becomes the mutated monster on the loose movie à la *The Blob.* Victor Shakopopolous was Allen's name in *What's New, Pussycat?*

Story 7: What Happens During Ejaculation? Sidney goes on a dinner date and has a romantic interlude on the back seat of a car. This information is analysed in Sidney's brain by Tony Randall, and motor control is commanded by Burt Reynolds. The emotional and sexual aspects of the encounter are treated as scientific mechanisms. Allen is a sperm waiting for orders from Emission Control - penis erection and ejaculation are treated as though launching a rocket. Allen worries about all the things that can go wrong. What if she is on The Pill? He could smash his head on a rubber wall. Worst of all, it could be a homosexual encounter. If he is masturbating, Allen thinks he is liable to end up on the ceiling. Allen is launched, and his mission is successful - he fertilises an egg.

Background: Diane Keaton and Woody Allen got into bed one evening and saw a late-night TV show discussing a new book by Dr David Reuben called *Everything You Always Wanted To Know About Sex (But Were Afraid To Ask).* Someone said Woody Allen was the only person who could film it. Allen got a copy and found it was a book full of questions and answers. He thought it would be a fun subject, bought the rights from Elliott Gould, and provided his own unique answers to seven of the questions.

The fourth episode was originally going to be What Makes A Man A Homosexual? It was the story of a spider, Allen, who attempts to seduce a black widow, played by Louise Lasser. After he succeeds, she eats him. We zoom out to see Allen as a homosexual scientist observing this encounter. The sequence was filmed but not used because Allen did not like the ending.

The Verdict: The problem with multi-story films is that each story is judged individually, and such films are usually judged by their weakest link. In this case, the Sodomy, Transvestite and Ejaculation episodes are far superior to the others. 3/5

Sleeper (1973)

Director Woody Allen, Writers Woody Allen & Marshall Brickman

Cast: Woody Allen (Miles Monroe), Diane Keaton (Luna Schlosser), John Beck (Erno Windt), Douglas Rain (Voice Of Evil Computer), 87 mins

Story: Miles Monroe, part owner of the Happy Carrot Health Food Restaurant in Greenwich Village, has minor ulcer surgery, which runs into complications, so his cousin has him frozen in suspended animation until they can find a cure. Two scientists thaw him in 2173 because they need an unregistered citizen to overthrow the government. This is not a nice future - it is akin to Aldous Huxley's *Brave New World*. On the run from the state, Miles poses as a robotic valet and kidnaps his 'owner' Luna, but he is caught and brainwashed. Meanwhile, ignorant Luna is politicised by the rebel underground and involves Miles in the uprising. Luna and Miles pretend to be doctors and are required to clone the state leader from his nose - all that is left after an assassination attempt. Miles holds a gun to the nose and threatens to shoot him between the eyes.

Subtext: The story's theme is in the title - sleep is a metaphor for non-commitment in both political and emotional life. This is about people waking up. Miles has to wake up to his political and personal responsibilities, and he wakens Luna to hers. She wanted to wake up but did not know it - this is indicated by her love of a poem about a caterpillar who transforms into a butterfly. When they first meet they are both wearing masks - Miles in his white face disguise (a human trying to be robotic), and Luna in her green face cream (robot trying to be human).

Background: Allen had an idea for a four-hour film in two parts. The first half would be set in contemporary New York, and then the central character was frozen. There would be an intermission, and then the second half would be set 500 years into the future. It was almost like a throwback to the old double bills that Allen used to enjoy as a child. United Artists loved the idea but it proved too big a writing job for Allen. He asked Marshall Brickman to co-write it, and they concentrated on the second half of the story. Allen used to appear in cabaret with Brickman, who played bass and guitar. They wrote by walking the streets, having lunch and dinner, talking all the time (just like a scene in a Woody Allen movie). Allen would then go off and write the script since he had to say the lines, then presented it to Brickman for his comments. They went on to collaborate on *Annie Hall*, *Manhattan* and *Manhattan Murder Mystery*.

As is normal for dystopian stories, this film warns against loss of personality, individuality and vulnerability. Only this dystopia actually looks quite nice - a result of the laid-back Colorado and California locations. And the music is also very pleasant - the soundtrack is courtesy of the Ragtime Rascals, Allen's jazz band.

This is an exuberant visual film, a slapstick comedy, which harks back to the silent movies: it features police chases like the old Keystone Kops, there is a giant banana, when a nose is run over by a steam roller it becomes paper thin and massive, and Miles' robotic disguise looks uncannily like Harry Langdon.

Here is some trivia for you: film director Joel Schumacher was the costume designer; Phil Ramone of The Ramones was Music Recordist; Douglas Rain aka HAL 9000 in *2001: A Space Odyssey* was the voice of the Evil Computer, and the French title was *Woody Et Les Robots*.

The Verdict: Funny from top to bottom - there is no chance of anybody falling asleep through this one. 4/5

Love And Death (1975)

Director Woody Allen, Writers Woody Allen & Mildred Cram & Donald Ogden Stewart

Cast: Woody Allen (Boris), Diane Keaton (Sonja), Féodor Atkine (Mikhail), Yves Barsacq (Rimsky), Lloyd Battista (Don Francisco), Jack Berard (General Lecoq), Henry Czarniak (Ivan Grushenko), Despo Diamantidou (Mother), Harold Gould (Count Anton Ivanovitch), Jessica Harper (Natasha Petrovna), 85 mins

> "Human Beings are divided into mind and body. The mind
> embraces all the nobler aspirations, like poetry and philosophy,
> but the body has all the fun."

Story: Boris Dimitrovitch Semyonyovitch Grushenko, Russian peasant, is forced to fight against Napoleon when all he wants is the love of his sweetheart Sonja Petrovna Pavlovna Volkonska. She grants his wish and marries Boris on the eve of a duel, believing that he will die. He survives. Halfway through the film they consummate the marriage, so that is the love half dealt with. Sonja decides they should assassinate Napoleon. They fail, and Boris is sentenced to die. He dies. That is the death bit.

Subtext: The mind thinks of everlasting love, but the body will die. Allen makes the practical point, one that reappears in his films, that philosophical and literary discussions mean nothing without a real life to back them up - the basic appetites for food and sex must be sated first. This is shown through the character of Sonja who, from the outside, is beautiful and cultured. But she is a cold, calculating woman, more interested in the intellectual, the spiritual and the sensual, than real life. She is the bad side of the mind, a mind which cannot enjoy life.

As in *Sleeper*, here Allen plays a sensitive, moral, misfit in another time, who makes references to contemporary culture, much in the fashion of Bob Hope, who made knowing quips to the audience in films like *Monsieur Beauclaire* and *The Great Lover*. As in Allen's other films, this breaks with the convention of the fourth wall. (Allen wrote a few sketches for Hope early in his career.)

At the beginning, Boris fears his own mortality but by the end of the movie, he has learnt to accept it. He even dances joyfully as death leads him off, and I do not think you can get more joyful than that. In this film, Allen is trying to show that art is fun, not dour as if to prove Malraux who said that Art is "the last defence against death."

Background: Allen planned to do a murder mystery set in New York - he even wrote it up. But he did not feel it was strong enough, so he went for the Russian philosophical angle. Echoing the giant Russian literary works of Fyodor Dostoyevsky (*Crime And Punishment*) and Leo Tolstoy (*War And Peace*), *Love And Death* was filmed in Paris and Budapest with a French crew. For a serious backdrop, Allen wanted the music of Stravinsky, but it was too heavy, so he used Prokofiev's score from Eisenstein's *Alexander Nevsky* (1938).

As usual, there are many references to other films. We see soldiers as sheep like the workers portrayed as sheep in Eisenstein's *Strike* (1924) and Chaplin's *Modern Times* (1936). Death with a scythe comes to visit like in Bergman's *The Seventh Seal* (1956). The lion statue becoming exhausted is a parody of the lion statue 'awakening' in Eisenstein's *Battleship Potemkin*. And Allen's fighting with his own loose, wilting, goosing sword echoes Charlie Chaplin in *Soldier Arms* (1918) and *The Great Dictator* (1940). The references were not constrained to film. One of Boris' monologue in jail mentions seven of Dostoyevsky's novels, talking about his characters in the manner of a gossip.

The Verdict: Of all his out-and-out comedies, this one is perhaps the most accomplished, because it has the confessional air of Allen's stand-up, but it also flirts with serious matters. 4/5

At the death, the only thing one can ask about comedies is: are they funny? The answer is yes. After seeing *Love And Death*, one does not immediately think about the conflicts between mind and body. After seeing *Bananas*, one does not consider one's political beliefs. In a similar vein, after viewing *Sleeper* one does not think about awakening one's emotional life. The problem with comedy, especially the broad comedy that Allen practises in these films, is that they are ultimately not thought-provoking. They are perceived purely as an entertainment.

Woody Allen was about to enter another stage in his life. He had been writing prose and one-act plays and scripts which showed a more serious aspect of his thoughts. It was now time for him to make a serious film.

Denying Death

Allen's first straight acting role was in Martin Ritt's *The Front* (1976), playing middleman Howard Prince. Set in the era of McCarthy's House Un-American Activities Commission, Zero Mostel's character finds himself blacklisted. The only way he can earn a living as a writer is to have a front, somebody who will pretend to have written the work, and take a cut of the money. Howard Prince is such a man, a loser who is only too glad to take credit and money for other people's work. A small man - his actions only make him smaller.

Emboldened by this role, Allen embarked on *Annie Hall*, the story of a death-obsessed man falling in love with a woman who loves life.

Annie Hall (1977)

Director Woody Allen, Writers Woody Allen & Marshall Brickman

Cast: Woody Allen (Alvy Singer), Diane Keaton (Annie Hall), Tony Roberts (Rob), Carol Kane (Allison), Paul Simon (Tony Lacey), Shelley Duvall (Pam), Janet Margolin (Robin), Colleen Dewhurst (Mom Hall), Christopher Walken (Duane Hall), Jonathan Munk (Alvy Aged 9), Marshall McLuhan, Dick Cavett, Jeff Goldblum (Lacey Party Guest), Beverly D'Angelo (Actress in Rob's TV Show), Tracey Walter (Actor in Rob's TV Show), Sigourney Weaver (Alvy's Date Outside Theatre), Truman Capote (Truman Capote Lookalike), 93 mins

> "I was in analysis. I was suicidal as a matter of fact and would have killed myself, but I was in analysis with a strict Freudian, and if you kill yourself they make you pay for the sessions you miss."

Working Title: Anhedonia

Story: The film starts with a character we assume to be Woody Allen doing his monologue to camera. He then becomes Alvy Singer who announces that "Annie and I broke up." He begins sifting the relationship through his mind, remembering or misremembering conversations and incidents as they occur to him in a stream of consciousness fashion. Alvy is a neurotic comedian who, after meeting Annie Hall, sees her change from country mouse to accomplished singer. Their affair ends, then resumes, and finally ends when Annie moves to Los Angeles to further her career. In the end, Alvy writes his first play, about Annie and him, and gives it a happy ending for him.

Subtext: Rather than separate the persona from the real Woody Allen, this film seems to forever cement the two in people's minds. The reason for this? Well, Woody Allen starts his routine, telling jokes in the opening scene and we are not sure whether it is Woody Allen or his character Alvy Singer. Alvy is a comedian, like Allen. Allen and Keaton were lovers, like Alvy and Annie. Diane Keaton was born Diane Hall but changed her name because there was already an actress under that name. Allen was Keaton's mentor as Alvy is Annie's. Keaton dressed in her own clothes for the filming. All these coincidences begin to make one wonder: what is real, and what is fantasy? In fact, Alvy makes the comment that he always had a problem distinguishing fantasy from reality. This is further complicated when you find out that just as Alvy and Rob call each other Max in the film, the actors Allen and Roberts also call each other Max in real life (a joke which is repeated in other Allen films).

The central theme of *Annie Hall* is the one of the creator and his creation. It is the *Pygmalion* story, where the artist falls in love with his own creation, then loses her when she begins to live her own life. However, part of the process of breathing life into his creation is making her aware of death. When Annie is in a bookshop trying to find a book, Alvy suggests she reads Ernest Becker's *The Denial Of Death*. This book, which Allen seems to have taken to heart since its ideas recur in his other movies, says that all of man's activities are a fight against inevitable death (although some people choose not to fight it, just accept it). As Allen said, "Any man over 35 with whom death is not the main consideration is a fool."

Becker says that art is a way of transcending mortality because an artist controls the lives and deaths of his characters. So, in *Annie Hall*, Alvy denies the death of his affair with Annie by writing a play in which her love continues to live for him. It is after free-spirited Annie realises that death is a way of life that her art, singing, becomes important to her and she becomes an artist in her own right. Art compensates for the limitations of life. By extension, if we follow this idea through, this means Allen denies death by writing and directing films.

Another aspect of the *Pygmalion* story is that Alvy is unable to accept Annie as his partner and as his equal. He is unable to tell her his feelings, to say that he loves her. Being unable to express emotion and to give some sort of commitment is also a male thing. As a result, Alvy becomes a little unlikeable and sad because he prevents himself from being happy. This is all part of the Woody Allen persona, and still holds true for films like *Bullets Over Broadway*, *Celebrity* and *Sweet And Lowdown*, where the persona is played by other actors.

Themes and ideas recur: Alvy mentions the difference between the body and the brain; Alvy says that Annie is polymorphously perverse – she can be aroused by every part of her body, like the model in *Celebrity*; Alvy hates television – while in LA, Annie comments on how clean it is, and

Alvy replies, "They don't throw their garbage away, they use it to make their TV shows"; the empty frame with no characters is used for the first time when Alvy and Annie are breaking up, to show how disjointed they are; life is perfect in art, but not in life, as in *The Purple Rose Of Cairo*; guilt as a motivational force.

In the end, Alvy and Annie remain good friends. In real life, Allen and Keaton broke up but remained lifelong friends – her opinion about his movies is the one he respects the most.

Background: Truman Capote has a walk-on - he appears as a very good imitation of Truman Capote. The film introduces us to a couple of new movie faces - Jeff Goldblum is one of the guests at a Hollywood party, and Sigourney Weaver is Alvy's new date waiting outside the cinema.

Having relied heavily on music for his early films, Allen chose a quieter soundtrack for this film. There is no music other than from source - radios heard in the background, Annie singing etc. Perhaps this was influenced by Bergman, who did not use music, or perhaps not. The titles were also a standard typeface, simply the title of the film and nothing more - another 'Bergman' touch, and one which Allen retains to this day. He says he does it because it is cheap, but this understated approach does not announce the subject matter to the audience, so helps make the viewer curious to find out exactly what kind of film it is going to be.

Annie Hall is an important film for Woody Allen for two reasons. First, Allen had reached a personal plateau where he could put his previous films behind him (although he never dismisses them, he certainly has little time for them) and clear the way to go on to make deeper and more personal films. Secondly, Allen met cinematographer Gordon Willis, an artist who became Allen's technical teacher, and showed him how films could be made. They would go on to make the next seven films together.

The Verdict: This is a great film to watch and let swim through your mind. It is so free form and loose that you get lost and do not see the construction. In this sense, it is like his earlier comedy movies. However, the content is completely different – here is a mature look at a relationship that shows how love can remain as people change and move on. The scene of Annie and Alvy's first meeting at the tennis court, their mad drive through traffic, and the drink on the terrace with subtitles of their real thoughts is one of the great scenes from Allen's movies. 5/5

Interiors (1978)

Director & Writer Woody Allen

Cast: Kristin Griffith (Flyn), Mary Beth Hurt (Joey), Richard Jordan (Frederick), Diane Keaton (Renata), E G Marshall (Arthur), Geraldine Page (Eve), Maureen Stapleton (Pearl), Sam Waterston (Mike), Henderson Forsythe (Judge Bartel), 89 mins

> "I was thrown out of there during my freshman year, for cheating on my metaphysics final. You know, I looked within the soul of the boy sitting next to me."

Story: Eve is a mother who decorates everything in black, white or grey (her family wears grey at her birthday party in her honour). She does interiors. Everything is cool, formal, aesthetic. She controls her environment, tells her children what to do (when she visits Joey & Mike she rearranges their furniture & decor, picks fluff off Joey's bathrobe) and even 'created' her husband Arthur by putting him through law school. Eve gives Mike and Frederick scents she prefers because she dislikes the ones they presently wear. She is a cold, intellectual (she is proud of Renata because she is a best-selling poetess), manipulative woman - a darker version of Sonja from *Love And Death*.

She fails to see her family as people because she moves and arranges them like objects. They have minds (interiors) of their own but feel they have to suppress their thoughts in her presence. The reason for this is Eve's fragile mind - she has had electro-shock therapy - and the family does not want to harm her. Eve uses this as a way of getting what she wants - a passive-aggressive attitude that recalls other Allen movies like *Husbands And Wives*.

So it comes as something of a surprise when, one morning, 63-year-old lawyer Arthur quietly announces over breakfast that he is leaving Eve for a 'trial separation.' (He is both hero and villain - hero for standing up for himself, villain for 'abandoning' his wife.) Eve tries to commit suicide.

Eve has three daughters (Chekhov's *Three Sisters*?) who echo the three ways, according to Ernest Becker, that man tries to transcend his limited, mortal self if he lacks faith in God: sensuality, romance and art. Flyn, the film and television actress, is sensual and beautiful, but her outward glamour hides inner turmoil. She does drugs. When Frederick tries to make love to her, he says, "You only exist when you are being looked at." Joey is the romantic. As Renata says, she has, "all the anguish and anxiety of a creative soul with none of the talent." Joey drifts from one dream to the other without achieving any of her ends. (She tries photography, writing, acting.) Because of her belief in the romantic, when her father announces he is leaving her mother, Joey is the one who suffers the most, who feels for her mother and resents her father. Renata is the artist/creator, able to produce poetry and a child, but this 'gift' isolates her from her husband (Frederick), a writer who feels inferior to her, and from the rest of the family because almost by definition an artist must be flawed/different. Renata has a feeling of impending doom, that death is all around her.

Interestingly, all three men (Arthur, Mike, Frederick) are warm, likeable characters who have been chilled/distorted by Eve and her daughters.

Arthur eventually finds Pearl, a life-affirming, joyful, colourful character, a two-time widow. (Where Eve is mind, Pearl is body.) Arthur and Pearl are married, watched by the impassive daughters. Eve turns up that night, then walks into the sea to drown. Joey goes in after Eve, but fails to save her mother. Joey is pulled out by Mike, unconscious. Pearl does mouth-to-mouth on Joey, breathing life into her (as she had done with Arthur).

After Eve's funeral, Joey and Renata embrace. The three sisters gather at the beach house and look out the window. "The weather's so calm," Joey comments. "Yes, it's very peaceful," Renata replies.

Subtext: This is about creativity. Eve is the most creative of all the characters. Despite her fragile mind, and her separation, she continues to remake the world in her aesthetic image. The colour schemes, the vases, the wood, the sofas all combine to create a unified whole. Eve herself is a work of art - her hair style, her clothes, her position within the environs she creates are all carefully co-ordinated. (These calm exteriors are in contrast to the fiery interiors of the characters.) It is only at the point when her greatest creation, Arthur, destroys himself by marrying the "vulgarian" Pearl, that Eve decides to create no more.

Flyn feels she is creating nothing of substance, that it is all image and no content. She also knows that this will only last a few years while she still has her looks. Her creativity is pointless.

Joey cannot find a way to express her creativity. After the death of her mother (the source of her anguish), Joey begins writing a diary of remembrances - so perhaps now she has found a way to be creative.

At the beginning, Renata feels that she is impotent (a very unusual word for a woman to use), that she cannot write anymore, that she cannot see the reason why she should create, that she constantly thinks of death, is terrified of it, of its intimacy, and immediacy. (She thinks of death when she looks at nature - the branches of trees, the crashing waves.)

Pearl is the personification of transformation. She brings a new colour into their lives. She wants to redecorate the beach house - something the others would not dare to do. She accidentally knocks over and breaks one of Eve's carefully placed vases - to Joey's consternation. All the men are attracted to her joie de vivre. But Pearl is not unaware of her effect on the daughters, which is why she is more complex than they give her credit for.

The film is an ensemble piece, but Joey is the character who is changed most by the story. With the rejection of her mother by her father, and then the death of her mother, Joey undergoes a transformation. Her romantic view of life is eroded, then shattered. She wants to abort her child with Mike - she distrusts/rejects the role of motherhood. Also, she wants to be creative so refuses the idea of becoming a copywriter for an advertising agency. She loves her mother, and wants her approval. But Eve only approves of artists (i.e. Renata) and Joey is not an artist - this explains Joey's need to be creative, and her antagonism towards Renata. Joey holds the same elitist/intellectual views as her mother - Joey says that Pearl is a "vulgarian" because Pearl does not know intellectual references and only goes on gut feeling/emotion. Joey becomes more human - she remains pregnant, she becomes a copywriter. Talking to Eve after the marriage, Joey explains that Eve is too perfect, too controlled, too perverse in her attitude to life and that she Joey feels anger/rage towards her. Despite it all, Joey still loves her mother.

And this is the thing - Arthur and the daughters love Eve and want to protect her, no matter how remote or intellectual or fragile or awkward she may be.

Visual Ideas: Visually, this is one of Allen's most beautiful and controlled movies. The beach house is all greys and creams. It is soulless and cold. Rigid. An ice palace. We always see the characters inside a room, looking out - never outside, looking in. This is a symbol of the interior lives of the characters, who all desperately seek release from the intellectualism of Eve.

Visual metaphors are used throughout. Among all the greys and creams comes Pearl, a woman in startling red. The red is used as a symbol - when Arthur tells Eve that he has met someone else, Eve overturns red candles. Whereas the movements of the others are still and smooth, Pearl's are quick, jagged, expressing her inner emotions. The interior of the beach house is serene, controlled, but the exterior is the crashing of large waves onto the beach - chaos and death are just outside the door. At the end of the film, when Eve is committing suicide, the beach is bleak/bleached, but we cut back to the other characters sleeping in warm oranges - this symbolises how the characters will become more human and emotional once Eve has disappeared from their lives.

Sound Ideas: It is very quiet and calm for much of the time, but this hides emotional ferocity. When Arthur and Eve meet for the first time after the separation, they talk in a civilised manner, then cut to an unbearably loud unrolling of black tape as Eve seals her room so that she can gas herself.

Similarly, in church, when Arthur tells Eve he wants a divorce to marry Pearl, suddenly we hear the crash of candles being overturned by Eve. Finally, after Arthur has married Pearl, we go from the interior quiet of the beach house to the external crashing waves as Eve walks into the sea to drown herself.

Background: With the financial and critical success of *Annie Hall*, Allen decided to go the whole hog and write and direct something which was as serious as serious could get. *Interiors* has the austere surface and emotionally intricate qualities of both Bergman and Chekhov.

At one stage, Allen was going to call the film *Windows*, because it features people looking out of windows, but *Interiors* won the day. Gordon Willis later went on to direct his first film, and called it *Windows*.

Upon release, *Interiors* garnered a mainly negative press in the US, but Allen was Oscar-nominated for best director and original screenplay, and Geraldine Page was nominated for her performance. Allen based the character of Eve on Louise Lasser's mother.

This film was unusual for Allen because it was the first he wrote which is told from the point of view of women. It also featured one of Allen's long line of formidable mothers: Colleen Dewhurst played a strong mother in *Annie Hall*, then came Geraldine Page in *Interiors*, Maureen O'Sullivan in *Hannah And Her Sisters*, Elaine Stritch in *September* and Gwen Verdon in *Alice*. When asked about this shift, Allen explained that at first he always wrote from his point of view because it was an extension of his monologues as a stand-up comedian. Then living with Diane Keaton influenced the way he thought, he wrote *Annie Hall*, and he began to write for women because actresses seemed to give stronger performances of his writing.

The Verdict: A cold, sombre piece, a great drama, and totally unlike any of Allen's other films. It deals with Allen's major themes (creativity, death) in a responsible manner. Exquisite. 5/5

Manhattan (1979)

Director Woody Allen, Writers Woody Allen & Marshall Brickman

Cast: Woody Allen (Isaac Davis), Diane Keaton (Mary Wilke), Michael Murphy (Yale), Mariel Hemingway (Tracy), Meryl Streep (Jill), Anne Byrne (Emily), Tisa Farrow (Party Guest), Helen Hanft (Party Guest), 96 mins

> "You don't get suspicious when your analyst calls you up at three in the morning and weeps into the phone?"

Story: Isaac is a 42-year-old man who is seeing 17-year-old Tracy. He sees it as an enjoyable but ultimately impossible match. Isaac's best friend is Yale, who has been married to Emily for 12 years. Emily has been talking about having children but Yale is more interested in the affair he is having with Mary. Isaac, on the other hand, is worried about what his ex-wife is going to write about him in her book about their marriage break-up - she left him for another woman.

At an art exhibition, Tracy and Isaac meet Mary and Yale - whatever Isaac likes, Mary dislikes and vice versa. Mary and Yale have even invented their own little Overrated Academy where they have placed Lenny Bruce, Gustav Mahler, Norman Mailer, Heinrich Böll, Vincent Van Gogh and Ingmar Bergman. Mary particularly dislikes Bergman, saying that she outgrew all that 'God's Silence' stuff in adolescence. Isaac is happy to part as soon as possible, complaining to Tracy that if Mary had said one more bad thing about Bergman he was ready to pop her one.

Isaac, a successful TV comedy writer, gets angry at the way his material is performed, says that it is not funny, and the only reason people are laughing is because, "This is an audience raised on TV - their standards have been systematically lowered over the years." Isaac quits his job and immediately regrets it - the loss of earnings means he has to find a much cheaper apartment in which to begin his novel.

At a benefit party, Isaac meets Mary and they start talking. He finds out she married her teacher, Jeremiah, an incredible intellect, and incredible in bed too. They walk all night and talk about his novel, and watch the sunrise on a bench by the Brooklyn Bridge. On the weekend, Yale cannot meet Mary, so she rings Isaac to go walk in Central Park. It rains, there is a thunderstorm and they end up in the Planetarium, pitch black, on the lunar surface. Isaac says that he thinks the brain is the most overrated organ. "Nothing worth knowing is understood by the brain." They are close together, in the dark.

Tracy tells Isaac that she has the opportunity to go to London to study acting. Isaac, both attracted to Mary, and feeling that Tracy is missing her life by being with him, encourages her to go, and he grants her a special wish for that night - they ride in a carriage around Central Park.

Yale breaks up with Mary and then, at the racket club, suggests that Isaac goes out with Mary. Isaac spends the evening with Mary. In the cab, he chats her up - "You look so beautiful, I can hardly keep my eyes on the meter." They make love.

Isaac meets Tracy outside her school, and she gives him a harmonica as a present. Isaac breaks off with her, saying that in London she will meet lots of actors and directors her own age. Tracy just cries.

Life with Mary is great for Isaac, until his ex-wife's book comes out, revealing all to the world, and then Mary announces that she is still in love

41

with Yale. Meeting Yale, Isaac cannot understand how this has happened. Isaac has tried to live his life with personal integrity and morality, and he ends up like this. Yale's only reply is that, "We're just people."

Time passes slowly for Isaac, trying to write his novel. He lists all the things that make life worth living and includes Tracy's face. He rings her but there is no answer. He runs to her apartment and catches her on the way to the airport - she is leaving for London. Isaac says that he made a mistake, that she was the one for him all along but he did not know it. Tracy is going, but she will be back. Isaac is afraid she will find somebody else. "Six months is not too long," Tracy consoles him, "You've got to learn to have a little faith in people." Isaac smiles.

Subtext: People are so worried about all the wrong things in life, the negative things, that they fail to see the good staring them in the face. This is represented by Isaac falling for Mary, with all her attendant intellectualism and neuroses, and by his insistence in reliving the past (his marriages), rather than cleansing himself and facing the future (Tracy). In other words, Isaac must reinvent himself, as the city is constantly being reinvented. The new coexists with the old. (We have constant references to art, old and new, to old buildings like the Brooklyn Bridge, and the new buildings being constructed - Isaac even says to Mary, "The city is changing," when they see the sun shining through the girders of a new building.) The old must embrace the new - literally in Isaac's case.

Tracy is an interesting character because she is the only one without neuroses. When they are shopping, she says that the reason Mary said stupid things was because she was nervous. When they are in Isaac's new apartment, she accepts that this is where Isaac is rather than complain about the noise or the water. Tracy is a calming influence - she may be only 17, but she is far more level-headed and adult than any of the other characters, except maybe Emily.

Isaac's idea for his novel puts forward another view, that people are busy creating problems for themselves so that they do not have to deal with the bigger issues of the universe. (The idea is echoed in *September*, where Lane must "keep herself busy" so that she does not have to deal with life.) This is illustrated by images of small people in the big city (Isaac and Mary in front of the Brooklyn Bridge, or walking through the universe in the Planetarium). Tracy's youth reminds Isaac of his mortality, which is mentioned several times. Also, she has integrity, something he is trying to retain despite his flaky and facile friends - only Isaac does not recognise that Tracy has it as well.

Isaac's opening line of dialogue, "Talent is luck; you've got to have courage," links in with Tracy's closing line, "You've got to learn to have a little faith in people," in that they are both talking about taking action on instinct rather than logic. Although reluctant, Isaac constantly makes changes in his life based on feeling (quitting his job) or on logic (breaking up with Tracy), using his moral code to reason his decisions. In the end, he smiles because he has at last realised that he and Tracy have the same point of view.

Background: This is a love letter to the city of New York, an idealisation. From the very beginning when we hear Gershwin's *Rhapsody In Blue*, and see Willis' images, the whole city just comes alive. It is always moving. Isaac, Yale and Mary are constantly walking and talking, whereas Tracy and Emily are mostly stationary in their conversations. Each scene is shot in a different location, emphasising the diversity and range of the city which never sleeps. People talk intimately on the streets, but in their apartments they are alone or separate from the world - Allen uses walls and doors to split the screen into sections, to show the characters cut off from each other and the world.

Each image in the opening montage was carefully selected, then the team heard about the fireworks over Central Park, so the crew were dispatched to hang out of the bathroom window of one of the production people's apartments to take the shot. Also, the end confrontation between Yale and Isaac was originally shot as a telephone conversation, but it was not working, so Marshall Brickman made them confront each other in a classroom in front of a grinning skeleton.

This is the first of Allen's films to be shot in both black and white, and widescreen. It was an experiment, and when it was finished, Allen was very unhappy with it. He even offered to do a free movie for United Artists if they did not open it. Thankfully, wiser minds prevailed.

Whilst filming *Manhattan*, Allen talked to Liv Ullmann, who said that Ingmar Bergman was visiting New York and they arranged to have dinner together. They talked and talked, Allen surprised at the similarities in their experiences.

The Verdict: From the opening moment, you are in. The music, the images, the movement, the dialogue. This is a big movie about little people. It is both expansive and intimate. Over the years, critics have complained about Mariel Hemingway's acting but quite frankly, I do not see the problem - I think she is very good. She is the quiet centre of Isaac's life, only he does not realise it. The point of the movie is that she stays in the background - the first close-up she gets is when she cries, which is the first time Isaac realises how real she is. 5/5

43

Stardust Memories (1980)

Director & Writer Woody Allen

Cast: Woody Allen (Sandy Bates), Charlotte Rampling (Dorrie), Jessica Harper (Daisy), Marie-Christine Barrault (Isobel), Tony Roberts (Tony), Daniel Stern (Actor), Amy Wright (Shelley), Helen Hanft (Vivian Orkin), John Rothman (Jack Abel), Anne De Salvo (Sandy's Sister), Joan Neuman (Sandy's Mother), Ken Chapin (Sandy's Father), Robert Munk (Boy Sandy), Sharon Stone (Pretty Girl On Train), Jack Rollins (Studio Executive), 91 mins

> "I don't want to achieve immortality through my work, I want to achieve it by not dying."

Story: In a train, there is a ticking like a bomb. The passengers are depressed, stern, unsmiling. Sandy looks across to another carriage and sees the passengers are bright, cheerful, laughing - a beautiful blonde blows a kiss at him. Sandy realises he is on the wrong train and desperately tries to escape it, but cannot get off. The depressed passengers walk through a garbage dump, and then we see the happy passengers from the other train also at the dump. The film stops, and the film executives declare that Sandy is not funny anymore. Where are the jokes?

Successful comedy film-maker, Sandy Bates is surrounded by horrible business people. He complains that since his friend Nat Burnstein died he does not feel funny anymore. There is so much human suffering, matter is decaying, and soon none of them will exist.

Sandy spends a weekend at the Stardust hotel where a retrospective of his movies is being shown. People are always looking at him, giving him gifts, but mostly wanting: autographs ("You're a master of despair"), interviews ("I'm doing a piece on the shallow indifference of wealthy celebrities and I'd like to include you"), money (charities), a job (actors and writers with CVs), sex (a woman is in Sandy's bed - her husband drove her all the way from Bridgeport and would be so proud if...).

As all this is going on, Sandy is slowly breaking down, depressed, remembering his childhood (as a boy magician, dressed as Superman and flying), and mostly his love for Dorrie (meeting her on a beach she says, "I'm fascinating but trouble," their tempestuous affair, her jealousy, her abuse as a child, her mental instability). To recapture Dorrie, he picks up Daisy, a classical musician. At the same time his current love, Isobel, leaves her husband for Sandy, and brings her two children. And the studio executives want to recut and change his film, substituting the garbage dump for a jazz heaven.

After taking Daisy out to the cinema, the car breaks down, and they end up at a UFO party. Sandy meets the aliens, who are in hot air balloons, and asks them questions. They advise him to tell funnier jokes. He is shot by a fan and dies. At his memorial service, a shrink says that people do not want too much reality in their films. Accepting this posthumous award, Sandy says that he had one perfect moment - it was with Dorrie, on a Spring morning, listening to Louis Armstrong play *Stardust*, watching her watching him. The audience asks why comedians turn out to be so sentimental.

Sandy is not dead - he collapsed. He moans, "Dorrie," and Isobel leaves him. Chasing after her, getting on the train he says he has come up with an alternative ending for the film, where the guy loves the girl, says sorry, she forgives him and there is a sloppy kiss. Isobel kisses him.

The film ends and all the actors are in the audience commenting on the making of the movie. His father says, "From this he makes a living?" Sandy looks up at the screen, walks out and the lights dim.

Subtext: One character says to Sandy, "Your films are all about people with personality disorders." This is the story of a man who sees the world in a distorted fashion. He is attracted to a dangerous personality and to unusual people, and his life is in complete turmoil, constantly interrupted by fans and employees and hangers-on wanting something from him. At the Stardust hotel the retrospective is an assessment of his work, whilst Sandy assesses his life. It is all about control: "You can't control life, only art. Art and masturbation. Two areas in which I'm a master." Sandy is losing control, like Dorrie lost control.

The fascinating, dangerous woman who is also mentally unbalanced is a character who recurs in Allen's movies. Dorrie is the first to make it on screen and, in part, she comes from Allen's second wife Louise Lasser. In the end, Sandy is afraid of becoming Dorrie, of breaking down like her. There is a chilling series of full-face jump-cuts of Dorrie talking directly to us. "I can't feel anything," she says. Having a breakdown is a way for Sandy to not feel any pain anymore.

Sandy realises that relationships are based on luck, and he is lucky to have Isobel. Eventually, he kills his old self, his immaturity, and is reborn as an adult - he takes responsibility for Isobel and her children. Sandy also thinks he is lucky to live in a society that puts a value on jokes, otherwise he would not be in the position he is in.

In a recurring theme, when Sandy and Daisy come out of seeing *The Bicycle Thieves*, Sandy explains that the bicycle represented survival for a working-class man, but middle-class people concern themselves with dying, love, sex, the meaning of life and other things to while away their time on this Earth. In the film within the film (the art which Allen controls), the central character realises that death is the only option (the passengers of both trains end up at the garbage dump) but he can enjoy life while he has it.

In this film about film, we have to ask, is the film we see the film the artist wanted us to see? Is the happy ending his ending, or the producer's? The point is that we are an audience, distracted for 90 minutes from our problems in the world. Allen distracts us by telling us not to think about death. Ironically, by doing so, we think about death.

The playful, surreal nature of this film-within-a-film is reminiscent of the work of Fellini, whilst the idea that it is better to make films that make people laugh echoes Preston Sturges' *Sullivan's Travels*.

Background: The film is full of unusual faces, to show the weird hallucinatory aspect of the story. To find these people, a notice was put in the newspaper and thousands turned up. Someone presented him with a giant zucchini - an incident which was used in the film.

Whilst filming, every morning for nearly a week Allen and Willis dragged everybody out to the same location at 8.00am and stayed until 11.30am, just to get one shot. But Allen and Willis thought it was too sunny, even though they were filming in black and white. While waiting, the crew played cards, or ball, and sometimes Allen would join them. There was another time when they wanted twilight and overcast - that shoot lasted almost a week also. The total shooting time was somewhere around 6 months.

The Verdict: Surprising at every turn, the visual and verbal narrative is quick and requires great concentration. The effect is very stimulating, startling at times, but it lacks the emotional punch of some of his other films.
4/5

Comedia De La Muerte

"Intellectuals are like the Mafia. They only kill their own."

Having discovered that he could write and direct introspective movies, Allen stepped back from the abyss for a while to be a bit more playful. He had also begun a relationship with Mia Farrow, who would influence his artistic life for the next 10 years.

A Midsummer Night's Sex Comedy (1982)

Director & Writer Woody Allen

Cast: Woody Allen (Andrew Hobbs), Mia Farrow (Ariel Weymouth), José Ferrer (Professor Leopold Sturgis), Julie Hagerty (Dulcy Ford), Tony Roberts (Dr Maxwell Gordon), Mary Steenburgen (Adrian Hobbs), 88 mins

"There is more to life than we perceive with our five senses."

Story: Professor Leopold Sturgis, an intellectual who thinks that "Nothing is real that cannot be experienced," is about to be married to freethinker and intellectual Ariel Weymouth. They are invited to a weekend party at the country house of Andrew and Adrian Hobbs. Andrew is a stockbroker ("I handle their money until none of it is left") and crackpot inventor who is having problems with his marriage - for some reason Adrian cannot make love to him. Also invited is sexually active Dr Maxwell Gordon, who invites Dulcy Ford, an equally randy nurse, to be his escort.

As soon as all the guests arrive, they begin to spark off one another. Andrew wants to be with Ariel, with whom he almost had an affair years earlier - "The saddest thing in life is a missed opportunity." Dr Maxwell, who proclaimed "Marriage for me is the death of hope," finds himself hopelessly in love with Ariel. When he is rejected, he tries to shoot himself. Adrian asks Dulcy advice about sexual technique, and learns about the Mexican cartwheel. Leopold is attracted to the instinctive, animal, primitive, Neanderthal lust of Dulcy. There is a comedy of errors, a roundabout of lovers and a resolution, all aided by one of Andrew's inventions: the spirit ball.

When Andrew and Ariel try to make love, they discover they do not love each other, that they were in lust. Leopold becomes crazy with jealousy, believing Maxwell is having an affair with Ariel, and shoots Maxwell with an arrow. Then, as though shot through with cupid's arrow, Maxwell declares his love for Ariel and she responds. Adrian tells Andrew that the reason she could not make love to him was because she felt so guilty about making love to Maxwell, his best friend - they make love. Leopold makes love to Dulcy and dies in the process. Then, via the spirit ball, his essence is transformed into a ball of light and he joins other souls in the woods.

Subtext: Yet again, Allen examines the mind, body and spirit, but this time it is wrapped up in a more whimsical setting. At the beginning, each of the characters are equally matched: mind/intellect (Leopold and Ariel); body/sex (Maxwell and Dulcy); sin/guilt (Andrew is guilty of unrequited love, Adrian of lust).

The central question the characters ask themselves is, "Are lust and love separate?" Maxwell is a lusty man, but he is converted to love. Andrew, who says "sex alleviates tension and love causes it," believes that he is in love with Ariel and finds out it is lust. Love works in mysterious ways. In the case of Professor Leopold, he believes in an intellectual meeting of the minds, but finds himself more interested in a meeting of the bodies, reverting to a primitive state. Leopold draws blood and likes it.

It is also a film about the rational man of science (philosopher, doctor, stockbroker, inventor) confronted by the irrational (love, spirit world, the afterlife). "I did not create the world, I only explain it," Leopold says at the beginning. By the end, he cannot explain his transformation from intellectual (mind) to primitive (body), and from primitive to essence (spirit). Similarly, Maxwell is transformed from a man who believes in lust, to a man who believes in love - again his initial hypothesis that "Marriage is the death of hope," is proved wrong. For Andrew and Adrian, the message seems to be that lust and love are not separate, but are both needed to balance a successful relationship.

Allen's continued use of magic and film is combined here in the form of the spirit ball, which is both magical (because it works independently of Andrew), and projects images (what people want to see, their dream fantasies). Andrew says that it allows us to see the unseen world, which is exactly what film does. To further this analogy (and why not), the film is often framed with characters outside the frame so that we only hear them. They are 'unseen' but at the same time by talking they reveal the truth. Also, much of the action (for example, when the characters make love, or Andrew crashes his latest flying machine) takes place outside the frame of the film.

Background: *Zelig* and *A Midsummer Night's Sex Comedy* were made at the same time. Allen finished writing *Zelig* and, whilst it was in pre-production, wrote *A Midsummer Night's Sex Comedy* in two weeks. Then he started casting, finding locations and filming both at the same time, doing chunks of one and then chunks of the other.

By the end of the shoot, the leaves were turning brown and yellow, so the leaves were painted green. When the film crew left, the Rockefeller Estate, who owned the property in the Pocantico Hills, complained because it did not want the trees green in winter. The green paint was dye, and difficult to get out, so some of the crew went back to paint the trees brown. Then, when the rains came, the brown paint was washed off and the trees were green again, in the middle of January.

It was exactly the kind of picture designed to keep American audiences away. Along with *September*, it was Allen's biggest financial disaster.

The Verdict: This is a pastoral comedy, a turn of the century mixture of sex and science which, if it had been made by René Clair in the 30s, would now be considered a wistful film of merit. Since it was made in 1982, audience expectations are different, and attendances were lower. Still, it is far from dull (the photography is stunning), and not without its attractions. 3/5

Zelig (1983)

Director & Writer Woody Allen

Cast: Woody Allen (Leonard Zelig), Mia Farrow (Dr Eudora Fletcher), Saul Bellow, Susan Sontag, 79 mins

> "Are you in analysis?"
> "Yes, I have been for the past 13 years."
> "And what has the analyst done for you?"
> "He's agreed with me that I need treatment. He also feels the fee is correct..."

Alternative Titles: The Cat's Pyjamas, The Changing Man, Identity Crisis And Its Relationship To Personality Disorder

Story: Leonard Zelig is the human chameleon. He is so afraid of standing out from the crowd that, not only does he take on the mannerisms of the people around him, he begins to look like them as well. Ironically, in the 20s, he becomes a cultural phenomenon, a personality who even has songs written in his honour, and there is a dance called the Chameleon.

This documentary traces the life of Zelig from his first mention in the diary of novelist F Scott Fitzgerald, to photos with playwright Eugene O'Neill, and appearances as a baseball player, gangster and black musician. Zelig, a clerk, goes missing, but is eventually tracked down as a Chinaman and put under the medical care of Dr Eudora Fletcher. She tries to get to the root of Zelig's psychological problems, literally his "unstable make-up." Zelig undergoes a series of tests. Hypnotised, he reveals he feels safe when he is like others and that he just wants to be liked. Ironically, his ability to be like others marks him out from the crowd.

Seeing an opportunity to make money, Zelig's half-sister Ruth takes him out of hospital and parades him like a freak, charging admission, licensing clocks, games, earmuffs, books and even dolls with multiple heads. Songs based on him include *Leonard The Lizard* and *Reptile Eyes*. On a tour of Europe (the French intellectuals find in him a meaning for everything), Ruth and her lovers are killed in a crime of passion and Zelig disappears. He is found later by Pope Pius, and Eudora takes him to her country home for treatment. Under hypnosis, he is free to express his opinions, and reveals his love for her. While he is awake Zelig pretends to be a doctor. Eudora says she is pretending to be a doctor and becomes his patient (thus empowering him). When he is examined by Eudora's bosses, Zelig is so opinionated that he starts a fight over the weather.

Zelig is cured, but he is still famous. He advises kids that they have got to be themselves. But, as with all celebrities, his words are adopted by everybody to mean what they want them to mean. As Eudora and Zelig plan to marry, he finds out that he was married before, when he was a chameleon. Everybody turns against him, blaming him for everything, and the scandal prompts him to disappear, to blend in with the crowd.

Eudora hunts for him, and finds Zelig in Germany, as part of Hitler's movement. They escape by plane, Zelig adopting Eudora's flying skills when she is knocked out. Ironically, his talent, his curse, saved their lives. After a Presidential pardon, Zelig and Eudora marry and live the rest of their lives together.

Subtext: The 30s were a time when everybody was deciding whether to become a Communist or a Fascist, both large movements who required people to become one of the crowd, to join for the collective good. Zelig is a man who wants to conform. He will give up everything - his identity, his integrity, his humanity - to be accepted. This is a fundamental Jewish condition, to assimilate. Allen warns us that if people do not stand up for themselves and their individuality, they will lose every freedom they have.

America is not portrayed as a meltingpot, where all races and creeds are accepted: the Klu Klux Klan considers Zelig a threat because the Jew could become Black or an Indian; the Christian spokesperson wants to "lynch the little Hebe" because of his immorality; and he is bullied by anti-Semites. If everybody just went along with these bullies, then the world would be full of good people doing bad things - Allen is showing us how the Nazis came to power, and how easily it could also happen in America.

Background: Allen wrote the complete script, then looked for archive footage to fit the documentary style. When he found something he liked, he would rewrite. To film new sequences, Allen's crew used 20s and 30s camera lenses, and the same lighting. They scratched the film. There were only two or three trick shots in the movie. Amateurs were used in the speaking parts, so that they sounded natural and not like actors. Allen would misdirect them to get realistic reactions and confused faces.

The Verdict: Like *Manhattan*, this is the story of how the integrity and love of a good woman can change a man. It is also one of Allen's most perfectly realised films - the documentary format and parody thereof is superb. Unusually, Allen places events in a real political context, which gives his message extra depth. This film works on so many levels as love story, parody, comedy, political and social comment, that it is difficult to explain it all in such a short space. 5/5

Broadway Danny Rose (1984)

Director & Writer Woody Allen

Cast: Woody Allen (Danny Rose), Mia Farrow (Tina Vitale), Nick Apollo Forte (Lou Canova), Sandy Baron, Corbett Monica, Jackie Gayle, Morty Gunty, Will Jordan, Howard Storm, Jack Rollins, Milton Berle, Joe Franklin, Howard Cosell, Danny Aiello, 88 mins

> "Nothing funny has ever happened to me on my way to the theatre. My life is not a series of amusing incidents."

Story: At the Carnegie Deli Restaurant a group of stand-up comics are entertaining themselves with stories, mostly about Danny Rose, the worst talent agent ever to hit Broadway. His acts include a blind xylophone player, a one-legged tap dancer, and a one-armed juggler – he drew the line at Barney Dunn, a stuttering ventriloquist. They settle down, as the best Danny Rose story is told…

Danny manages Lou Canova, a bad lounge singer who had a hit in the 50s. Lou is a hit with the ladies, and finds himself on the brink of a comeback. Danny arranges with Milton Berle for Lou's performance at the Waldorf to be an audition for Milton's show. Lou is married with kids, but he's infatuated with Tina Vitale, to whom he has been sending one white rose every day. Danny disagrees with this behaviour – "As my Grandmother used to say, God rest her soul, 'You can't ride two horses with one behind.'" Anyway, Danny is to act as the beard, to bring Tina to the show as his girlfriend, only Tina has an argument with Lou and will not go. Danny goes after her, meets her friends in organised crime, one of whom is in love with Tina. They think that Danny Rose is the one sending the white roses, and start a vendetta – Danny Rose must die. On the run, Danny and Tina begin to talk.

Tina believes that you must live for the moment and get everything you can out of life, regardless of the consequences for others. Danny believes that guilt is important, that you must be responsible for your actions. Also, that you must suffer to appreciate life. He quotes his uncle, God rest his soul, who believed in, "Acceptance. Forgiveness. Love." Running, they go through flatlands, get on a boat to cross the Hudson River, and make it back to Danny's apartment.

Tina thinks back to a few weeks previous when she arranged for a new, powerful manager to come and take over Lou's career. In the meantime, Tina, who likes interior decorating, suggests how Danny could improve his room – he encourages her, says she has talent, that he has faith in her, that he sees her decorating embassies. He gives her confidence in the same way as for his acts.

Danny and Tina are caught by the Mob. Danny persuades them that he is not Tina's lover and names Barney Dunn (who told Danny he had a job on a cruise, so would be unreachable). The gangsters leave Danny and Tina tied up while they go check. Danny, remembering the advice of a magician he once managed, says they just have to wiggle and the ropes will become loose. (Danny enjoys Tina wiggling against him.) They run for it, are shot at in a hangar full of balloons for the Thanksgiving Day parade, and escape.

Returning to Lou, they find him drunk a half hour before his big night – Danny sobers him up, Lou is great, and then Danny is told he is being dropped. Danny is shocked and despondent. When he finds out that Barney Dunn was not on the cruise, but was beaten up, Danny goes to visit him and promises to pay all his hospital fees.

Lou leaves his wife and lives with Tina, but Tina is not happy. She leaves Lou and, at the Thanksgiving Day Parade, decides to go see Danny. Danny is having a party for all his acts, serving them frozen turkey dinners, when Tina arrives asking for forgiveness. Danny says he cannot. He thinks about it, runs after her, and takes her back to the party. He had accepted his loss, now he forgives her, perhaps in the future, he will love her.

Subtext: Again, Allen talks about guilt and the way it plays with the mind and body, stopping Tina living her life. She sets herself up as being hard and tough – she wears dark glasses, she talks aggressively, the Mob are her friends – but she lacks confidence and direction (she visits a fortune-teller to get advice). Tina also sets up a protective barrier by pretending that nothing hurts her, that she hurts people before they hurt her. Only, she has integrity, and Danny is the one who brings it out of her.

Background: At one point Danny shows Tina a photo of him and Frank Sinatra, only he is not in the photo somewhere. Mia Farrow used to be Mrs Frank Sinatra. Also, Sinatra once played a singer who betrays his agent in *Meet Danny Wilson* (1951).

The Verdict: This is great. The mannered performances (Allen with his square glasses and gesticulating arms, Farrow with her big hair, dark glasses and tough voice) and light comedy tone completely mask the serious intent. Then, the pay-off ending at Danny's Thanksgiving Party is a real gut-wrencher. Allen is playing the most dangerous game in writing and film, making comedies which are also tragedies - a subject also dear to the heart of Charlie Chaplin. Here Allen succeeds beyond all expectations. 5/5

The Purple Rose Of Cairo (1985)

Director & Writer Woody Allen

Cast: Mia Farrow (Cecilia), Jeff Daniels (Tom Baxter/Gil Shepherd), Danny Aiello (Monk), Stephanie Farrow (Cecilia's Sister), Van Johnson (Larry), Milo O'Shea (Father Donnelly), Dianne Wiest (Emma), Glenne Headly (Hooker), 84 mins

Story: The film opens, ironically, with the song *Cheek To Cheek*, and the words "I'm in Heaven..." Cecilia, a waitress in Depression-era America, is married to Monk, who has been unemployed for two years and has accepted his fate. Monks neglects Cecilia, treats her like dirt, occasionally beats her. Cecilia escapes from this reality through her love of the movies. She watches *The Purple Rose Of Cairo*, a romantic adventure story set in the white apartments of Manhattan and the dusty ruins of Egypt.

When Cecilia catches Monk with another woman, she leaves, but eventually returns when she finds she has nowhere to go. Then she is fired from her job, and spends all day watching *The Purple Rose Of Cairo*. One of the characters, Tom Baxter, looks at her, says she must really like the movie because she has seen it five times, and walks out of the screen to talk to her. While Tom and Cecilia talk in an amusement park, the characters left in the movie sit around and argue because Tom was the lynchpin of the plot.

The film's Hollywood producer, Raoul Hirsch, learns of this disaster, and tells actor Gil Shepherd that he must control his own creation. Shepherd flies to New Jersey, meets Cecilia and tries to persuade his character Tom Baxter to return to the silver screen. Nothing doing. Tom and Cecilia have fallen in love. Tom learns about poverty, reproduction and religion ("God?" he says, "You mean like the writers of the film?")

Shepherd and Cecilia begin talking about his career, and he takes her out for the day, buys her a ukulele, they sing in a music shop, whilst Tom is picked up by a hooker and taken to a brothel. Tom enthuses to the women about the miracle of childbirth and, enchanted by his sweetness, they decide to give him a freebie. Tom refuses, saying that he only loves Cecilia and will forever remain faithful to her.

Since Tom's film money cannot buy anything in the real world, Tom takes Cecilia into the movie – they drink, dine and dance at all the best places in Manhattan.

Returning to the film theatre, the real world, Cecilia has to choose between Tom or Shepherd – they both say they love her. She tells them, "I have to choose the real world." Heartbroken, Tom returns to the movie. As Cecilia packs her bags again, she argues with Monk, who tells her, as so often before, "You'll be back." She waits at the cinema and finds that Shepherd has returned to Hollywood without her – the real man was false and the false man was real.

Cecilia sits with her bags in the cinema, crying. As she watches Fred Astaire and Ginger Rogers dance on the silver screen, we hear the song *Cheek To Cheek*, and the words "I'm in Heaven..." Eventually Cecilia becomes engrossed in the film and begins to smile.

Subtext: One of the pleasures of going to the cinema is to escape from reality. This film, like many of Allen's movies, plays with the idea of film, and what exactly is fantasy and reality. It also plays with the nature of creation – is the artist responsible for their own creation or not? And celebrity – if Gil Shepherd cannot control his image then his career is in jeopardy. Ultimately, it has one message: Art is perfect, life is not.

But then, when you look at the world of art, it is not so perfect. Inside the movie, the champagne is actually ginger ale, the characters are scripted so they do not have any freedom of choice. Even when Tom escapes into the real world he cannot make any decisions other than those written into his character. The film characters are reliable because they do the same thing over and over - one patron even complains that she saw the film the previous week and they are not doing the same things. So, in real life, are people any less set in their ways? They have choices, but do they make any? And what happens when Tom makes an unscripted decision by leaving the film? The other characters do nothing but wait around – and the audience waits around, looking at them. One is reflecting the other.

So, the world of art(ifice) only appears perfect. In fact, art only reflects real life.

The only character who makes an active choice is Tom Baxter, and he inspires Cecilia to make the same leap of faith.

The Verdict: This is a gentle comedy that has some fine scenes (the best being Tom Baxter in the brothel) and an interesting idea, but the characters are too weak to hold the flimsy material. Although Jeff Daniels does well in his double role, the main problem is that we never really get to know Cecilia – her background, her motivation – and she remains two-dimensional at best. 3/5

Hannah And Her Sisters (1986)

Director & Writer Woody Allen

Cast: Barbara Hershey (Lee), Carrie Fisher (April), Michael Caine (Elliot), Mia Farrow (Hannah), Dianne Wiest (Holly), Maureen O'Sullivan (Norma), Lloyd Nolan (Hannah's father), Max Von Sydow (Frederick), Woody Allen (Mickey), Julia Louis-Dreyfus (Mary), Julie Kavner (Gail), J T Walsh (Ed Smythe), John Turturro (Writer), 103 mins

Story: Divided into sixteen sections, where each expresses the point of view of one of the characters, we follow the lives of Hannah and her sisters.

Financial advisor Elliot is married to self-sufficient Hannah, but he lusts after her sister, Lee, who is vulnerable and needs him.

Lee is living with an older man, Frederick, an artist, who has protected her from the world but, ironically, it is she who tells him about what is happening in the outside world.

Mickey, the hypochondriac TV producer (and Hannah's ex-husband), finds out that he may actually have something wrong with him and is wracked with existential angst. He once had the worst ever date in the history of the world with Hannah's other sister, Holly.

Wild and wacky Holly wants to be an actress, but never gets the job, always losing out to her friend April. When they start the Stanislavsti Catering Company, they both fall for David, an architect, who prefers April.

Hannah is completely self-sufficient and centred. Without realising it, her comments undermine Holly's self-confidence, and Lee is so overwhelmed by Hannah's perfection that she feels inferior to her in every way.

Lee and Elliot have an affair. As a result, Lee leaves Frederick, but Elliot regrets the affair because he realises it is Hannah he truly loves. After time, Lee and Elliot drift apart - Lee marries her professor at Columbia University.

After he is given the medical all-clear, Mickey realises that all life hangs by a thread, so he tries out all the religions to see which one has the best contract with God. Life is meaningless. After a failed suicide attempt, he wanders the streets, goes into a movie house to see a Marx Brothers film and laughs for the first time in a year. What if there is no God? There is no reason for that to ruin his life. He should enjoy the experience while he can.

Having tried acting, catering, singing - all without success - Holly tries writing and impresses Mickey with her script. They get together, marry, and Holly becomes pregnant.

Subtext: There is a quote from Tolstoy in the film that says life is meaningless - a sentiment repeated by Mickey. He ends up deciding he should enjoy what little life he has, which is the point of this film. *Recurring Ideas:* Three sisters à la Chekhov and *Interiors*; love is unpredictable; having children - Mickey's infertility is the reason for his marriage break-up with Hannah; New York - David takes April and Holly on a tour of Manhattan's architectural highlights; poetry - here it is e e cummings, in *Crimes And Misdemeanors* it is Emily Dickinson; Holly goes to the opera - Larry and Carol go in *Manhattan Murder Mystery*; psychoanalyst - Elliot talks to one; Holly is the artist without an art, like many of Allen's characters.

Background: The story of the sisters is drawn from fragments of Mia Farrow's family (her real-life mother, Maureen O'Sullivan, plays her screen mother), and her scenes were even filmed in her apartment. Hannah's self-sufficiency is also an attribute of Mia's. During filming, she kept asking Allen if Hannah was genuinely good, or whether she was manipulative, but Allen did not know. This ambiguity is captured on film. It would seem that Judy in *Husbands And Wives* is an exploration of the darker side of Hannah's character.

The Verdict: This is completely enchanting, from beginning to end. A romantic comedy, with the accent on the romantic, this is Allen at his most optimistic. However, just below the surface there is a bedrock of serious thought, which is why it works so well. 4/5

Radio Days (1987)

Director & Writer Woody Allen

Cast: Julie Kavner (Mother), Julie Kurnitz (Irene), Wallace Shawn (Masked Avenger), Seth Green (Joe), Michael Tucker (Father), Josh Mostel (Abe), Renée Lippin (Aunt Ceil), William Magerman (Grandpa), Leah Carrey (Grandma), Joy Newman (Ruthie), Dianne Wiest (Bea Fletcher), Farrow Previn (Andrew), Oliver Block (Nick), Maurice Toueg (Dave), Sal Tuminello (Burt), Kenneth Mars (Rabbi Baumel), Mia Farrow (Sally White), Tito Puente (Latin Bandleader), Larry David (Communist Neighbour), Danny Aiello (Rocco), Jeff Daniels (Biff Baxter), Tony Roberts (*Silver Dollar* Emcee), Diane Keaton (New Year's Singer), William H Macy (Radio Voice), Kenneth Welsh (Radio Voice), Woody Allen (The Narrator), 85 mins

Story: Told as a loose collection of anecdotes and remembrances about radio and the people who performed on it, we begin with two burglars breaking into the Needleman house. There is a phone call. The burglars pick up. It is a radio quiz show. They win. They steal $50 and ransack the house. The following morning a van arrives at the Needleman's full of the radio show prizes - they replace everything they lost with brand new things. We are introduced to Little Joe and his family - his mother and father (they can argue about any subject, even which is the best ocean), his Aunt Ceil and Uncle Abe (he is always bringing home fish from Sheepshead Bay), and his Aunt Bea (she is in search of a man to marry but always picks the wrong sort).

Little Joe listens to the Masked Avenger and wants a Masked Avenger secret compartment ring. When the Rabbi wants him and his friends to collect for the new state of Israel, Joe and his buddies steal the money but are caught. And that is how the Masked Avenger drove Little Joe to crime.

Joe often goes on trips with Aunt Bea and her beaus. With one he went to the Radio City Music Hall to see the film *Philadelphia Story* - he thought it was like entering Heaven. With another, Aunt Bea won a radio contest through her knowledge of Uncle Abe's fish and bought Joe a chemistry set. One beau left her stranded when they heard Orson Welles' *War Of The Worlds* broadcast. Another was married and would not leave his wife. Another was gay.

Uncle Abe loves listening to the *Bill Kern Sports Show*, and we hear about Kirby Kyle, the one-legged, one-armed, blind pitcher. Aunt Ceil on the other hand loves listening to a ventriloquist on the radio.

Little Joe, who collected many stories about the radio celebrities, tells the story of Sally White, a Brooklyn girl who started as a cigarette girl, got used by radio celebrities, witnessed a murder, was going to be killed but the mobsters got her onto a radio show instead, which is not aired, so she eventually takes diction lessons and stars in her own show as a gossip columnist.

The power of the radio is shown by the way people listen to the broadcasts of the war in Europe and the East, and by the nation listening to the reports on Polly Phelps, an eight-year-old girl trapped down a well.

The New Year is here, and all the radio celebrities gather at a club - the party is broadcast of course - and Little Joe's family listens. As the year passes, never to return, one of the celebrities muses that their time too will pass. Only Joe remembers them, and each year his memory fades.

Background: Hannah And Her Sisters was very successful, both critically and at the box office, which meant that he had a lot of money for his next picture. If you were to look at Woody Allen and ask yourself, "I wonder what he was like as a kid?" I think *Radio Days* would answer your question. Allen was brought up in Brooklyn and spent some of his youth at Coney Island, either in the famous amusement park or on the boardwalk. (Rollercoasters feature in *Annie Hall*, *Stardust Memories*, *The Purple Rose Of Cairo* and *Radio Days* so I guess the Coney Island ride was one he could not forget.)

Many of the incidents and details are true. On the other side of Woody's street, there was a family of Russian Jews and Communists. They shocked the largely Jewish neighbourhood by not observing Jewish high holy days. He got a chemistry set and dyed his mother's coat in an experiment - true.

Visually, the film has a bleached texture, which allows some of the reds and other strong colours to really come through. The colour tones for Little

Joe and the real world are dark, whereas all the people and sets for the radio world are brightly lit and sparkling. Some of the compositions are very reminiscent of Edward Hopper.

Subtext: Each character dreams of something they will never attain (Mother of romance, Father of money, Bea of a husband, Ceil of a night out at the Stork Club (which does not allow Jews), Little Joe of his Masked Avenger ring), but feeds vicariously off the experiences of the radio celebrities. By seeing the seedy way in which Sally White makes her way from Brooklyn obscurity to Broadway fame, we see how false the ideal of celebrity is.

The Verdict: This is a thin, whimsical tale with an enjoyable texture. The costumes, the sets, the period detail, the music are all wonderful to look at and listen to. Still, there is no real tale to hang the story on, other than the rags-to-riches tale of Sally. The family resolves no conflicts. It is a film of contrasts and ironies - the powerful voice of the Masked Avenger coming from a small man, the radio dishing out money and prizes like manna from heaven to people who have little or nothing. It is a sweet film, and certainly Allen's most autobiographical. 3/5

Death Rattle

> "Life is divided into the horrible and the miserable. Those two
> categories. Just be happy you're miserable."

Having spent 5 years working on some playful, mainly fantastical
projects, *September* represented a change in Allen's work. For the next 5
years, he would be embroiled in betrayal, death and infidelity. Allen was
asking himself why people stayed together when they caused themselves
and each other so much pain.

In 1987, Mia Farrow gave birth to Allen's first child, Satchel O'Sullivan
Farrow, and the importance of children began to make itself an issue in
Allen's work.

September (1987)

Director & Writer Woody Allen

Cast: Denholm Elliott (Howard), Dianne Wiest (Stephanie), Mia Farrow (Lane),
Elaine Stritch (Diane), Sam Waterston (Peter), Jack Warden (Lloyd), 82 mins

Story: At the end of summer, a group of people gather in a house and
talk. During this process, the women reveal their true nature to each other.

Lane lives in the house and has spent the summer recovering from an
overdose of pills. At the age of 14, she killed her mother's lover, a gangster.
Since then, her life has been hell. She plans to sell the house and move to
New York, perhaps to earn a living as a photographer. In fact, she is pursu-
ing Peter, with whom she is in love.

Peter is an advertising man who has spent the summer living in an outside room writing a novel, *The History Professor*, about his father. The
theme is survival - his father was blacklisted during the McCarthy era and
supported his family by playing poker and betting. However, Peter has
become interested in writing a biography of Lane's mother, Diane, another
survivor.

Diane is a famous old movie star who lived an exciting, dynamic life.
She left Lane's father, Richard, and went to live with Nick, a gangster who
beat her. Bigger than life, Diane is not ashamed of her reckless past, and is
still trying to live her life to the full.

Howard is Lane's older neighbour. When he finds out Lane is leaving, he
becomes jealous because he is in love with her. He gets on well with Steffi,
Lane's friend.

Steffi is married, but is presently having a trial separation from her husband. Since she arrived, she and Peter have been flirting, and it is only a

matter of time before they consummate the relationship. Steffi is only continuing the flirtation because she wants to be wanted.

Lloyd is Diane's husband, a quiet man, a scientist. He tells Peter that all space comes from nothing and goes to nothing. All is haphazard, morally neutral and violent. He holds onto Diane at night because love is vital - he holds onto life.

A storm brews, the electricity is cut, and things happen. Howard declares himself to Lane, but she loves Peter. Peter declares himself to Steffi, and they make love. Lane finds Peter and Steffi together. In the light of day, Diane decides that Lane cannot sell the house, that it is hers, that she wants to live the rest of her days there.

Lane's life is ruined. Her love is lost. Her plans are stopped. She has no life. She is nothing. In the ensuing argument, Lane accidentally reveals that it was her mother who shot Nick, and that Lane was told by the lawyers to take the blame for it. At this, Diane backs off, and Lane is given a chance at a new life.

Subtext: This is heavy stuff. Basically, Diane has no guilt for the crime she committed, not only against Nick but against her daughter. "Life's too short to dwell on tragedies," she says. Lane, on the other hand, is lonely, is not in love with someone who loves her, and the best she can hope for is to "keep busy" with the sale of the house and all the future distractions in New York.

Everybody loves the wrong person. Everybody's life is unfulfilled. Everybody has nothing to look forward to. As Diane says, "The future is missing."

Background: This production has an interesting backstory. Allen filmed and edited together a version of the film which included Charles Durning, Maureen O'Sullivan and Christopher Walken (who was later replaced by Sam Shepherd). He felt he had miscast some of the actors, so he dumped the film, recast, did a bit of rewriting, and reshot the whole thing. Denholm Elliott played Lloyd in the first version, but Allen thought he would be better as Howard in the second one.

The whole film is set in a house inspired by Mia Farrow's country house. The setting and the mix of characters is very reminiscent of *Interiors*, with Lane and Joey having similar goals and personalities - they are both artists without an art so they cannot express what is inside them.

The most intriguing aspect of this story is that it seems to be partly based on the death of gangster Johnny Stompanato (he was bossman Mickey Cohen's henchman), who beat up his girlfriend, actress Lana Turner, and was killed by her daughter.

The Verdict: This has a tremendous hook on which to hang its characters - a mother has an affair with a gangster who beats her, then kills him and lets her daughter take the blame. Of note is the roaming camerawork, and the unusual use of off-camera sound. However, both the studio set and the confessional dialogue give the impression that this is a play being filmed - this artificiality detracted from my viewing pleasure. The play (this is Chekhov, isn't it?) delivers less than it promises and fizzles out because the central focus, Lane, is underdeveloped. The acting, especially Stritch's, is first-rate, but doesn't save the film. 2/5

Jean-Luc Godard asked Allen to play the Jester in his film of *King Lear* (1987). Allen agreed and turned up at the appointed place one morning. Godard was in a bathrobe smoking a cigar, and he had a film crew of only three people. Godard simply told Allen what to do as they were recording. Allen is credited as playing the part of Mr Alien, the fool, and the other players were Norman Mailer, Burgess Meredith and Molly Ringwald.

Another Woman (1988)

Director & Writer Woody Allen

Cast: Gena Rowlands (Marion), Mia Farrow (Hope), Ian Holm (Ken), Blythe Danner (Lydia), Gene Hackman (Larry), Betty Buckley (Kathy), Martha Plimpton (Laura), John Houseman (Marion's Father), Sandy Dennis (Claire), David Ogden Stiers (Young Marion's Father), Philip Bosco (Sam), Kenneth Welsh (Donald), Bruce Jay Friedman (Mark), 84 mins

"We all imagine what might have been."

Story: Marion Post is a professor of German philosophy, and head of her department. She has turned 50. She is on her second marriage, to a heart doctor, Ken. She is on sabbatical, taking time off to write her latest book in a rented room. Whilst working, she overhears, through the heat ventilation, the confessions of a patient who is terribly depressed and thinking of killing herself. At first, Marion refuses to let this interfere with her work but then, after listening to this pregnant woman, Hope, she realises that all Hope's fears are her own.

There is a series of flashbacks and meetings. Marion learns that her brother Paul idolises her and hates her at the same time. She remembers a party before her second marriage, to Ken (they had an affair whilst his wife was in hospital), where Ken coldly discarded his first wife, telling her, "I accept your condemnation." She kisses Ken's best friend, Larry Lewis, who loves her - he says that she is all mind, no passion, that she is just like Ken and they deserve each other.

When Marion sees Hope, she follows and bumps into her childhood friend, Claire, an actress. Claire's husband is dazzled by Marion's wit and intelligence, and Claire asks her husband to look at her once in a while. Claire says she stopped their friendship because Marion flirts all the time, perhaps without knowing it. No one can compete with her.

Her stepdaughter, who loves her, says that Marion stands above people, evaluates them, judges them. Her brother says that when she criticised his writing she stopped him from writing - from that moment on he tried not to embarrass her. A former pupil says that Marion's lecture on Ethics And Moral Responsibility changed her life.

In a dream, her father says that he has only regrets: for not marrying the woman he loved; for driving his daughter too hard… Larry says that he included her in his novel, as Hlenka. Her first husband, Sam, her professor and mentor, killed himself 15 years after their divorce.

Marion does not sleep with Ken anymore. She asks him why. "I accept your condemnation," he says.

In a dream, she buys Sam a masque. She wears it, and he kisses her.

In an antique shop, Marion bumps into Hope staring at Klimt's painting of a pregnant woman, a painting called *Hope*. They walk and talk, Marion hoping to extract information from Hope. But Marion drinks, says that at 50 you look up and see where you are. Chances are gone that you can never have back, like having a child. She thinks back to her abortion - she was selfish, wanted a career, had her life ahead of her, a life of the mind. Sam, a much older man, the father, wept, asked her how she could do that without even discussing it with him?

Going back to her room, Marion hears Hope talking about her. Saying that Marion cannot allow herself to feel. She must have had a cold life. She pretends everything is fine, but really she alienates everybody close to her. She is afraid of feeling, even the feelings she may have for her own baby. Her life is empty.

At home, Marion talks to Ken and tells him that at lunch with Hope, Marion saw Ken with their friend Lydia. She knows they are having an affair. Marion is not angry, just sad that Ken is as lonely as her.

Work on the book goes well, without any distractions. Marion begins to read a passage of Larry's novel, to find out what he wrote about her. He said that, for a moment, he sensed intense passion beneath her cold exterior, and then the walls came down.

For the first time in a long time, Marion feels at peace.

Subtext: At the beginning, Marion explains her philosophy by saying, "If it's not broke, don't fix it." Of course, at this moment in time, she does not realise she is broke. In writing the book she announces she wants to "cut herself off from everything." She is already cut off from people. She is cold and intellectual. By taking an interest in Hope, she begins to warm up, become compassionate. In her mother's book of Rilke poetry, she recites the line, "You must change your life." On her voyage of self-discovery, navigated by Hope, Marion discovers what kind of person she really is. She decides to change her life, to become more of a human being, to let her emotions show.

Visually, this film is so delicately lit, so finely framed, that you feel it is a light pastry that will melt in your eyes. This is courtesy of Sven Nykvist. A recurring image is a series of doors through which Marion walks towards us, gradually getting closer.

Background: Allen had long had the comic idea of a man overhearing a woman's conversation, then acting on the information to become her fantasy man, and thus win her for himself. This was later used as the basis for *Everyone Says I Love You*, but it also served as the starting point for *Another Woman*.

One cold day, the crew spent two hours putting down the rails that would carry the camera for a long shot of Gena Rowlands. It was a shot to visually introduce her to the audience whilst we heard a voice-over. The crew finished, Allen said, "No," and they tore it up. He eventually introduced the character in her apartment, panning the camera around her photos, which showed us all the people we were about to meet in the film.

The Verdict: This is an intelligent film which shows a woman assessing her life, realising her mistakes, and about to take steps to correct herself. It is a positive film, beautifully played in a low-key way, and far better than I thought it would be. Like *Alice*, this is about transformation. I prefer *Another Woman*. 4/5

New York Stories: Oedipus Wrecks (1989)

Director & Writer Woody Allen

Cast: Woody Allen (Sheldon Mills), Julie Kavner (Treva), Mae Questel (Mother, Sadie Millstein), Mia Farrow (Lisa), Jessie Keosian (Aunt Ceil), George Schindler (Shandu, The Magician), Larry David (Theater Manager), Marvin Chatinover (Psychiatrist), Mayor Edward I Koch, 38 mins

Story: One of three stories in this anthology film (the other two are directed by Martin Scorsese and Francis Ford Coppola). Sheldon Mills is 50, a partner in a successful law firm, and still having trouble with his mother, Sadie. He dreams that he is driving her coffin to the cemetery, but still she gives him directions because she knows best.

Sheldon takes Lisa, his fiancée, to meet his mother and Sadie embarrasses him with stories about his bed-wetting. His mother advises him not to marry Lisa, who has three children. Next, Sadie turns up at the office, and embarrasses him in front of his boss. At a magic show, Shandu the Great puts Sheldon's mother in a box and shoves swords through it - Sheldon smiles. Then, Sadie disappears and the magician does not know where she went. After the initial shock has worn off, Sheldon feels relaxed and has the best sex he has ever had with Lisa.

One day, Sadie appears as a giant presence in the New York sky, always talking about Sheldon. He is on the TV news, and they talk about him wetting the bed as a child. Sheldon is mortified. (Mayor Ed Koch thanks Sadie for spotting criminals for the city.) At the suggestion of his analyst, Sheldon hires Treva, a medium, to help bring his mother back to normal but she fails. Unable to cope with all the media attention, Lisa and Sheldon quarrel all the time and break up. Sheldon loves Treva's cooking, and they get together. Sadie approves and so decides to come back down.

Subtext: Listen to your mother. She knows what is best for you. (And You always end up with a girl who is just like your mother.)

Background: Believe it or not, Jessie Keosian was Allen's biology teacher in school. Everybody on the set called her Jessie, except Allen, who could only call her Miss Keosian. Allen came up with the idea of doing the anthology film, which was originally to be done with Steven Spielberg, but Spielberg had to pull out and was replaced by Coppola.

The Verdict: A lovely little short. Not his best work, or deepest, but it is diverting. 3/5

Crimes And Misdemeanors (1989)

Director & Writer Woody Allen

Cast: Martin Landau (Judah Rosenthal), Claire Bloom (Miriam Rosenthal), Anjelica Huston (Dolores Paley), Woody Allen (Cliff Stern), Alan Alda (Lester), Sam Waterston (Ben), Mia Farrow (Halley Reed), Martin Bergmann (Professor Louis Levy), Jerry Orbach (Jack Rosenthal), Nora Ephron (Wedding Guest), 107 mins

> "I went into a store, I bought a rifle. I was gonna... you know, if they told me that I had a tumour, I was going to kill myself. The only thing that might've stopped me, might've, is my parents would be devastated. I would, I woulda' had to shoot them, also, first. And then, I have an aunt and an uncle, I would have, you know... it would have been a bloodbath."

Story: As Judah Rosenthal, a rich optometrist, is being honoured for his good works - the opening of a new hospital wing - he is surrounded by his family. Judah is nervous, not about his speech, but that his mistress of two years Dolores Paley will tell his wife Miriam about their affair. Judah consults his patient and friend rabbi Ben, who is slowly going blind - Ben says that Judah must confess to his wife and submit himself to her mercy. (Ben is optimistic and believes that people are basically good. Judah is a realist/cynical and believes that people are not good.)

Cliff Stern is a poor, unknown documentary film-maker who wants to produce a film about Professor Louis Levy, but is talked into making money by doing a film profile about his wife's brother - shallow, successful TV producer Lester. Cliff's marriage is breaking up, and he falls for producer Halley Reed, another deep thinker and lover of old movies.

Dolores threatens to reveal Judah's financial embezzlement and adultery. After much debate and soul-searching, Judah decides to save his own skin, and arranges for Dolores' murder through his hoodlum brother Jack. Judah is devastated when Jack tells him the deed is done - Judah washes his hands, he fears the wrath of God, then he goes to Dolores' apartment to collect any evidence that she knew him. Judah is wracked with guilt, visits his old home, and imagines a conversation about God and the meaning of life.

Cliff and his wife Wendy have dinner with Lester and Halley, Cliff constantly trying to keep Lester and Halley apart. When Professor Levy commits suicide, Cliff runs some of their filmed conversations, where Levy says that human beings need love to survive, that we invest the cold universe with warm emotions. Levy was alone and lonely. Cliff is without love, so he declares himself to Halley and kisses her. She responds, but Cliff's ethical dilemma is that he is married.

Cliff cuts together his film about Lester, comparing him to a fascist dictator and showing him using his position to seduce women - Cliff is fired. Then Halley leaves for a job in London - she will only be there for 3 or 4 months. Cliff says it will be like a prison sentence - cut to Edward G Robertson in prison in *The Last Gangster*.

Four months later, the family are at the wedding of rabbi Ben's daughter. Cliff and Wendy have split up, and Cliff is surprised to find Halley there, as Lester's new fiancée. Heartbroken, Cliff hits the drink, and is joined by Judah. They talk, and Judah tells the story of a perfect murder. In his story, Judah tells Cliff, the murderer awoke one day and realised that there is no God, that it is not a moral universe, that he is not punished, that people only carry their sins around with them if they want to. Judah leaves, kisses his wife, and is happy because he is in love. Cliff is not so happy, or content - he is in love, but he is not loved.

Background: The first thirty pages of a new script were written in Allen's New York workroom, which overlooks Central Park, and the rest was written on hotel notepaper whilst on a European tour. When that story was filmed and edited together, Allen decided to cut out a third of it (Cliff's affair with Sean Young, tracking Halley to find out who she is having an affair with) and rewrite/refilm. The result was a more focused and interesting film.

Subtext: Eyes, vision and watching are the main themes of the movie. The eyes of God are always upon us, according to Judah's father, and He sees all, knows all, and will punish the wicked. Judah is an eye-doctor, and his patient rabbi Ben is going blind. Dolores asks Judah if he thinks the eyes are the window to the soul and he thinks not. Later, when Dolores is dead, Judah looks into her dead eyes, and sees that there is no soul there. Cliff is a film-maker, so he sees everything through a camera. He is making a film about a philosopher (deep watcher?), but has to make money so he makes a film about a TV producer (people watch TV). Cliff loves watching films, either with his niece Jenny or with Halley.

The use of light is interesting - the characters are constantly moving from light to dark, and lights are turned on and off. Normally, we reveal our deepest thoughts, we confess, in the dark.

A sub-theme is the use and abuse of money - if you earn a lot of money, you also get fame, success, awards, recognition, as with Lester and Judah. If you have good intentions, you do not get money or celebrity, as in the case of Cliff and rabbi Ben.

Differences between reality and fantasy are shown with scenes from the film, and then scenes from other films. For example, Judah and Dolores quarrel, and then Carole Lombard and Robert Montgomery quarrel in Hitchcock's *Mr And Mrs Smith* (1941). Similar commentaries come from *Happy Go Lucky* (1943) and *The Last Gangster*. When Judah tells Cliff his perfect murder story, Cliff tries to add a ending like they would have in the movies.

Judah's story is about a man who thinks he believes in God, then finds out that God does not exist, so he will not be punished for his crime. Cliff's story, on the other hand, is about a man who believes in God, and finds out he was right, because he is punished for his misdemeanour. Professor Levy says that it is a cold universe, man invests it with emotions, and gives it a moral structure.

At the end, when Judah tells Cliff his story, Cliff tries to give Judah's story a moral structure, a 'movie' ending, but Judah says Cliff is wrong. There is no God. We define ourselves by our choices, and hope that future generations might learn more.

Professor Levy also said that human beings need love. Often, we seek to love someone who reminds us of our past, but we try to repair their mistakes. This contradiction, this tension between past and present, between reality and expectation, is what propels many of Allen's film couples.

The Verdict: This is a superb film in every department. The acting is controlled and concentrated. The story is simple but devastating. The subtext is serious but understandable. The whole film is summed up in the final image of rabbi Ben, now blind, dancing with his daughter at her wedding. We live in hope that the knowledge of our generation, and all the generations that came before us, will allow future generations to learn more. (As Cliff tries to educate his niece Jenny.) We set up religious systems to help control our universe, but we are all essentially blind, like the blind rabbi, a good man, trying to pass on his knowledge and wisdom to his daughter. 5/5

Alice (1990)

Director & Writer Woody Allen

Cast: Joe Mantegna (Joe), Mia Farrow (Alice Tate), William Hurt (Doug Tate), June Squibb (Hilda), Marceline Hugot (Monica), Dylan O'Sullivan Farrow (Kate), Julie Kavner (Decorator), Keye Luke (Dr Yang), Judy Davis (Vicki), Cybill Shepherd (Nancy Brill), Alec Baldwin (Ed), Blythe Danner (Dorothy), Gwen Verdon (Alice's Mother), Patrick O'Neal (Alice's Father), Bernadette Peters (Muse), Elle Macpherson (Model), Bob Balaban (Sid Moscowitz), 106 mins

"Hey, don't knock masturbation. It's sex with someone I love."

Story: Alice is the pampered wife of a rich stockbroker. He plays a lot of tennis and backgammon, attends a lot of functions and never plays with the children. She has her own personal trainer and interior decorator, her children are looked after, and most of her time is spent shopping, being made up, and being swept along by the latest fads and trends. She dreams of being kissed by Joe, a man who picks up his child at her children's school. Joe reminds her of Ed, her first love, a wild artist who died in a car crash. Alice gave up Ed and her career to marry Doug and now regrets it.

Complaining of a bad back, Alice goes to Dr Yang, an acupuncturist and purveyor of magical substances. He hypnotises Alice to allow her to release her mental anguish (which is causing the physical pain). Alice relives her time with Ed, proposes a liaison with Joe, spends a day with Ed's ghost, becomes invisible thanks to the good Doctor's herbs, and has an affair with Joe.

Joe goes back to his wife, and Alice discovers her husband has had a string of affairs. Dr Yang gives her a love potion that will make one of them love her - she can choose which she wants. She does not. She decides to leave her shallow life, gets on a plane to India to work with Mother Theresa, returns to Manhattan and brings up her children to have better values.

Subtext: This feels like a rerun of *The Purple Rose Of Cairo*, but instead of the Depressed 30s, we're in the Yuppie 90s. Alice feels she is wasting her life, and wants her fantasy man to make her life complete. Like characters in other Allen movies (*Husbands And Wives* and *Stardust Memories* come to mind), Alice bases her present love on a previous love - they are artists (Joe a saxophone player, Ed a painter). Like *The Purple Rose Of Cairo*, Alice chooses reality over fantasy. Unlike that film, she creates a new reality for herself.

Recurring Ideas: Dr Yang's reference to the head and the heart; rain, especially when Alice makes love to Joe; manipulation of time through voice-over and flashbacks; Joe, Alice and the children go to the circus; Alice is an artist without an art - she tries to become a writer; we see the characters through mirrors; psychoanalyst; love is unpredictable, irrational, has no logic; magic.

Alice tries to find meaning in her life by writing about it. She takes a course and her professor tells the class that prose novels deal with the internal and drama/TV/films deal with the external. This is the process by which they express themselves - the implication is that novels are more serious than films, which is patently untrue. In terms of subject, Alice's muse says that losers make the best subjects - Allen has spent a lifetime testing this theory.

Background: This film was tough to make because Allen wanted it to be stylish. There was no useable footage in the first week - on one occasion, when Mia walked through Central Park, her blood-red coat opened slightly, enabling us to see her white dress underneath, which ruined the shot for Allen. He reshot half the film, and rewrote the beginning and end before he was happy.

The Verdict: Although this is a handsome production, and it has many witty ideas, none of the characters really come to life. A film for a rainy afternoon when you have nothing else to do. 2/5

Shadows And Fog (1992)

Director & Writer Woody Allen, based on his play *Death*

Cast: Michael Kirby (Killer), Woody Allen (Kleinman), David Ogden Stiers (Hacker), Victor Argo (Vigilante), Mia Farrow (Irmy), John Malkovich (Clown), Madonna (Marie), Donald Pleasence (Doctor), Lily Tomlin (Prostitute), Jodie Foster (Prostitute), Kathy Bates (Prostitute), John Cusack (Student), Philip Bosco (Mr Paulsen), Josef Sommer (Priest), Kate Nelligan (Eva), Fred Gwynne (Hacker's Follower), William H Macy (Cop With Spiro), Julie Kavner (Alma), Wallace Shawn (Simon Carr), Kenneth Mars (Magician), 86 mins

> "I'm not afraid of dying... I just don't want to be there when it happens."

Story: A man is killed. Kleinman is woken in the middle of the night and told he must join the vigilante group, that he is an essential part of The Plan. Kleinman is frightened. The landlady gives him some pepper to throw in the face of the killer, and says, "I don't want them to find you in an alley with your throat cut from ear to ear." Kleinman reassures her, "Don't worry - he mostly strangles."

A circus clown talks to Irmy, his sword-swallowing girlfriend, after a performance - "Nothing is more terrifying than trying to make somebody laugh, and fail." Irmy wants a child but the clown says that, "A family - that's death to the artist," emphasising that an artist must be free. He then goes to visit Marie the trapeze artist and makes love to her, but they are caught by Irmy, who then packs her bags and leaves.

Kleinman visits the doctor to find out what The Plan is. Instead, Kleinman gets a drink and a tour of the dead bodies in the doctor's laboratory. The doctor says that the more dead bodies he examines, the more knowledge he will acquire. Eventually, when the killer is apprehended, the doctor hopes to dissect him, to find the true nature of evil. There is nothing spiritual about it, he explains to Kleinman. There is nothing for us after death.

Arriving in town, Irmy meets a whore, who takes Irmy off the dangerous streets and into the protection of the whorehouse. When Irmy says that she's a sword-swallower, one of the whores replies, "That's my speciality too." Sitting down, talking, the whores say that, "Unrequited love is the only love that lasts." Some students enter and Jack, a rich student, offers Irmy money for sex. She refuses so he ups the price from $20 to $700 and she accepts. Jack enjoys it very much, and Irmy says that it was real for her, she wasn't acting.

Kleinman sees the Mintz family, Jews, being arrested - they are being blamed for the killings. A priest assures Kleinman he is the right kind of Jew and will be okay. Whilst trying to put in a good word for the Mintz family at the police station, Kleinman finds out that the doctor is dead, and that they have proof of the killer's identity - a glass with fingerprints. Kleinman remembers his drink with the doctor. While Irmy is causing a commotion when being booked by the police for prostitution without a licence, Kleinman steals the glass. Meeting outside, they walk around together trying to find shelter. Kleinman sees his boss (a peeping tom) and is told he will not get a promotion. Then Kleinman finds he is being put on a list by the police and the priest. Kleinman's fiancée rejects him. He is accused of being disloyal by the differing vigilante groups. Finally, the police find the glass on Kleinman and he is accused of being the killer. He throws pepper in their faces and runs for it.

The clown arrives in town, without make-up, looking for Irmy. At a bar, he meets Jack and finds out how much Jack enjoyed having sex with Irmy. Jack says that Irmy is incredible, but from his point of view it is lust not love. Shocked, the clown does nothing. When he meets Irmy, he seems to appreciate her more. Leaving the town they come across the dead body of a woman - her baby lying nearby. They take the baby and, with Irmy's money, decide to settle down together.

At the circus, the clown holds the baby and is transformed - he wants more than one baby. He is no longer selfish, art is no longer everything to him. Then the killer chases Irmy, but Kleinman saves her, and draws the killer to the magician. The magician performs his mirror trick, trapping the killer in a chair of locks, but the killer escapes. Kleinman, who is an amateur magician, joins the circus and escapes into a new life. The magician says that people need illusions, like they need the air.

Subtext: Anything can happen in the night. Civilisation has gone, only the primitive world remains. But what happens to man when he realises, like the doctor and Jack, that there is nothing more than what we see? Irmy points out that we see the light from a star, not the star itself - the star may have died millions of years ago. Kleinman says that if we cannot rely on what we can see, what can we rely on? If he can see a chair, he must be able to sit on it. The Magician says that, "People need illusions, like they need the air." Each character has an illusion shattered during this night.

When Irmy first appears, she is wearing a costume and wig - taking them off, she reveals her true self. The clown is in make-up, then when he goes into town without costume and make-up he finds his true feelings for Irmy.

The sensual pleasures make life liveable: When the clown and trapeze artist start making love they talk about food. The whores give their clients drink before they have sex. Irmy drinks before having sex with Jack. Kleinman and the doctor drink surrounded by dead bodies.

Background: Allen has always been interested in the work of the German Expressionists, whether it is in literature, painting (he owns pieces by Oskar Kokoschka and Emil Nolde) or film. At one stage Kleinman says, "Schulz the tailor thinks that nothing exists at all and it's all in the dream of a dog," which refers to both Bruno Schulz, author of *The Street Of Crocodiles*, and a Franz Kafka short story. The photography is incredibly atmospheric as are the sets. Like *September*, the whole film was shot in a studio, to give Allen more control. This has the feeling of an old silent feature by the likes of F W Murnau (*Nosferatu*, *Sunrise*) or maybe even Fritz Lang (*M*).

The movement of the camera is much more daring than in previous Allen films. Instead of keeping the camera still, in the scene where the whores laugh about sex with men Allen has the camera revolving in the centre of the whores. Also, when the students enter, the camera becomes hand-held and shaky - the technique used in *Husbands And Wives*. When the killer claims the doctor, the camera moves out and then up and we see into the room where Irmy and Jack have made love - this re-enforces how near death is to us all.

One shot is a giant eye painted on a wall. Then you begin to notice that there are lots of these white eyes dotted around the film - the lights in the whorehouse, and on the streets, the moon and its reflection. We are watching the film, but it is also watching us.

Verdict: It would have been interesting if Allen had kept the original ending to the play, in which Kleinman is killed by Death. Only, that is an adolescent ending (as Mary Wilke points out in *Manhattan*). Allen is now a mature man who appreciates the joys of life, so although this film may not strictly adhere to the rules of the Expressionistic genre, it shows that at the end of every night, there is a sunrise to look forward to. 3/5

Husbands And Wives (1992)

Director & Writer Woody Allen

Cast: Woody Allen (Gabe Roth), Mia Farrow (Judy Roth), Sydney Pollack (Jack), Judy Davis (Sally), Jeffrey Kurland (Interviewer/Narrator), Bruce Jay Friedman (Peter Styles), Juliette Lewis (Rain), Galaxy Craze (Harriet), Lysette Anthony (Sam), Liam Neeson (Michael), Ron Rifkin (Rain's Analyst), Blythe Danner (Rain's Mother), Brian McConnachie (Rain's Father), Nora Ephron (Dinner Party Guest), 107 mins

> "A relationship, I think, is like a shark. You know, it has to constantly move forward or it dies. And I think what we got on our hands is a dead shark."

Story: Jack and Sally calmly announce to their best friends, Gabe and Judy, that they are separating. Judy, for some reason, is devastated by the news and it disturbs her for the rest of the evening. "Do you ever hide things from me?" she asks Gabe, and they talk about sex and attraction.

After many years of married life, Sally tries to adjust to single life but has some difficulty - when she goes on a date with an opera lover, she is constantly thinking of Jack and phones/argues with him several times. Jack, on the other hand, takes only three weeks to fall in love and move in with an aerobics instructor.

Gabe is impressed with the writing of one of his students, Rain, and they begin having serious talks about writing and creativity. Rain says how much Gabe's approbation means to her.

Judy is in love with her editor, Michael, (she gives him her poems to read) but she cannot have him because of her marriage. She matches him with Sally - romantic Michael is impressed by Sally but his feelings are not reciprocated. Sally is always nervous, hyper-critical, and literally running away from Michael.

When Jack finds out about Sally and Michael, he becomes insanely jealous and breaks in on them making love. In fact, Sally had not been enjoying the sex that much and her thoughts had been elsewhere.

Gabe's unpublished novel explains that there are many sperms and only one egg, which explains why men try to spread sperm around, and why women try to protect their eggs. The novel concludes that you should not expect too much out of life.

When Rain praises the novel, Gabe says how much her approbation means to him. She then loses the only manuscript in a cab, it is found, and in the mean time she explains that the novel is well written but the ideas are second rate. A transfer of power has occurred between Rain and Gabe.

Jack and Sally get back together, whilst Gabe and Judy split. Judy says that she must grow and change, whilst Gabe argues that to change is death to a relationship. Gabe moves out.

At Rain's 21st birthday party, a lightning storm cuts all the electricity. In candlelight, Rain asks Gabe to kiss her. Gabe is tempted to begin a relationship but he knows how it will end.

Judy declares herself to Michael, they argue, and somehow Judy persuades Michael to marry her. He thinks it was all his idea.

Subtext: Every question that Judy asks is a question she is asking herself. In the same way that she hides her poems from Gabe, she hides her true feelings and motives from everybody, including herself. As her ex-husband says, Judy is a passive-aggressive - she gets everything she wants by getting you to give it to her. She wants Michael, so she gets rid of Gabe. She keeps the apartment, of course.

Gabe does not have any problems, other than being attracted to self-destructive women. He pulls out of a relationship with Rain because he knows how it is going to end. At one point he says that "change equals death." By this, he means that, essentially, once things are stable and comfortable, we want things to remain the same (age, income, house, work). Gabe always wants unstable women (which is a sign of his artistic temperament).

Gabe asks the question, "Can passion be sustained in a relationship?" It begs the question, "When passion goes, what replaces it?" Companionship?

Sally and Jack represent Gabe's thesis in action. They are stable, then they break up, go a bit mad (freedom is frightening), and then end up together because they want stability and are willing to compromise a little to maintain the relationship. More than anything, they see marriage as a buffer against loneliness. Ironically, they have sexual problems, and the passion has gone out of their relationship, yet they are interviewed in bed.

Gabe is the only one who ends up alone.

Recurring Ideas: Gabe repeatedly loves the same personality type, the self-destructive woman; storm cutting electricity supply and so they use candlelight; the fantasy that single life is better than the reality of married life; unfaithful lovers and integrity. Also, the calm way Sally and Jack announce their separation is similar to the quiet way Arthur announces his separation from Eve in *Interiors*.

Background: The rough, documentary style of the camerawork and editing came from Allen's reaction to the prettiness and precision of modern films. Why not include only those actions and words which are important to the story - forget about sweeping cameras, precise colour etc. (Hold on, this is beginning to sound like Dogme95) Di Palma lit the sets, and Allen told his camera operator to get what he could, and if he missed it, or the actors were out of frame, not to worry about it. They all assembled in the room and filmed with no camera rehearsal. It was faster and, as a result, Allen came in under budget for the first time in years. He only had three days of reshoots. In the editing, Allen often jump cuts (same angle, different time) which creates a nervous, disjointed effect. (Similar to the shots of Dorrie's madness at the end of *Stardust Memories*.) The style of the film is as volatile as the events it portrays.

Yet, for all this seeming chaos, every single word of the film was carefully scripted. And the seeming roughness of the camerawork does have an overall plan. For example, when we first see Gabe and Rain they are in the classroom and walk out of the school. The next time they meet, they are outside the school and walking into the park. This steady linked progression of time and place continues until we reach Rain's kitchen and the birthday kiss. At the beginning, we are on Gabe's turf, but by the end we are in Rain's domain, echoing the change in power between the couple.

The Verdict: Some stunning performances from everybody, some clever camerawork and an incisive script make this an entertaining and thought-provoking film. Allen asks us what makes and breaks marriages, then shows us many intimate moments of truth as the characters discuss their options.

Allen has often suffered complaints from his fans, saying that they preferred his earlier, funny films. In the same way, Rain's parents say that they prefer Gabe's earlier, funny stories. Conversely, Rain complains that his novel is not serious enough, and he replies that he is "deliberately distorting it for comic effect." Allen has always tried to tread the fine line between comedy and tragedy - this may be his finest film. 5/5

Die Laughing

"Life doesn't imitate art, it imitates bad television."

When Mia Farrow and Woody Allen broke up, the whole world knew about it. Allen was accused of sexually abusing his adopted child, which was not proven, and he had restricted access to his natural born child. The relationship with Mia ended when it was discovered that Allen was having an affair with Mia's adopted daughter Soon-Yi Previn. Allen married Soon-Yi on 22 December 1997 and they have since adopted a baby.

Allen continued working throughout the court cases and hearings - finishing *Manhattan Murder Mystery* and writing *Bullets Over Broadway*. His writing and directing remain well-crafted - he is still in control of his art.

Manhattan Murder Mystery (1993)

Director Woody Allen, Writers Woody Allen & Marshall Brickman

Cast: Woody Allen (Larry Lipton), Diane Keaton (Carol Lipton), Jerry Adler (Paul House), Lynn Cohen (Lillian House), Ron Rifkin (Sy), Alan Alda (Ted), Anjelica Huston (Marcia Fox), 104 mins

Story: Carol and Larry Lipton are a comfortable married couple who start talking to their older neighbours, Paul and Lillian House. When Lillian dies of a heart attack, Carol begins to suspect Paul of murder and follows the clues, dragging Larry along with her. Their mutual friend, Ted, a writer who has feelings for Carol and wants to open a restaurant with her, is much more enthusiastic about the mystery. Larry works as a book editor, where he meets sexy Marcia Fox. She flirts with him, but Larry does not notice and is more concerned with fixing her up with Ted.

Carol and Ted track down Paul's girlfriend, model Helen Moss, and follow her to Paul's old cinema. The mystery seems over, then Carol sees the dead Lillian House on a bus, and tracks her down to a hotel. By this stage, Larry can see that Carol and Ted are getting too close, so he agrees to be more adventurous – he and Carol go into the hotel and find Lillian's body. They call the police, but the body disappears. They return later, find Lillian's body on top of the elevator, it goes dark, they get out through the basement, see the body being loaded into the back of a car, and follow it to a foundry where the body is disposed of. They see who did it – Paul.

Without a body as proof, they have nothing. Carol and Larry and Marcia and Ted meet, and Marcia works out what was done, and how to trap Paul. They trick Helen Moss, who is an actress, into recording dialogue for a part, then edit the words into a phone message for Paul. They pretend they have Lillian's body, and want money for it. Carol becomes jealous of Marcia, because Ted pays her a lot of attention, and she takes it out on Larry. Then Carol is kidnapped by Paul, and Larry comes to rescue her.

In the back of the cinema, *The Lady From Shanghai* is playing - the end shoot-out scene with the mirrors and the man with the bad leg. There are mirrors at the back of the screen (for the renovation), and Paul's faithful assistant, Mrs Dalton, has a bad leg. There is a shoot-out, mirrors are broken, and Mrs Dalton kills Paul.

Rescued, Ted and Marcia are together, and Carol is vibrating from the experience.

Background: When Allen was doing stand-up comedy he was friendly with his neighbours, and went away for six weeks. Upon his return, he knocked on his neighbours' door and the husband was standing there in his nice smoking jacket, very happy with himself. He informed Allen that his wife had died - she had fallen out of the window. Allen wondered why the guy did not seem too heartbroken. Had he killed his wife? In 1974, Allen wrote a murder mystery script with Marshall Brickman based around this idea, but he thought the plot too thin. Instead, they redeveloped the characters and it became *Annie Hall*. Allen wanted to make a comic film to offset the horrible things that were happening in his private life.

The colours in the film are bleached out greys and blues, almost as though Allen wanted to film in black and white, like one of the films noirs he emulates. *Manhattan Murder Mystery* cost somewhere around $14 million to make, and is one of his most popular recent films. Considering that a Hollywood film costs in the region of $40 million, Allen is good value for money.

Subtext: When you grow old physically, you do not have to grow old mentally. This is Carol's story – she is driven to do something with her life, to start the restaurant or solve a mystery. She almost gets involved with Ted, and ignores Larry, then becomes angry when she is no longer the centre of Larry and Ted's attention.

The Verdict: Unusually for Allen, there are some genuine moments of physical tension – when Carol sneaks into Paul's apartment, when they go into the hotel room and discover the body (both times), and the shoot-out at the end. This is a homage to *Double Indemnity*, *The Lady From Shanghai* and all the old films noirs of the 40s and 50s, and a pretty good one too. I liked it very much, but it does not have the emotional edge of his serious films. 4/5

Bullets Over Broadway (1995)

Director Woody Allen, Writers Woody Allen & Douglas McGrath

Cast: John Cusack (David Shayne), Jack Warden (Julian Marx), Chazz Palminteri (Cheech), Dianne Wiest (Helen Sinclair), Joe Viterelli (Nick Valenti), James Reno (Sal), Jennifer Tilly (Olive Neal), Rob Reiner (Sheldon Flender), Mary-Louise Parker (Ellen), Jim Broadbent (Warner Purcell), Tracey Ullman (Eden Brent), 98 mins

Story: "I am an artist, and I won't change a word to pamper a Broadway audience," says young playwright David Shayne. His producer, Julian Marx says that it is a rough world. Cut to Cheech and his hood friends nonchalantly blowing away some guys and then going for a bite to eat.

"No truly great artist has ever been appreciated in his own lifetime," David's friend explains, citing Van Gogh and Edgar Allan Poe as examples. He then asks David, "Which would you save if you rushed into a burning building and could only save one: an anonymous human being or the only remaining copy of the complete works of William Shakespeare?"

Julian makes a Faustian pact with a big-time mobster, Nick Valenti, who agrees to put up the money and let David direct his own play on Broadway but only if the mobster's bimbo has a major role. David agrees to sell his artistic soul, and in the first blush of worldly success succumbs to every other temptation he encounters, including an affair with his leading lady, the fading Broadway legend Helen Sinclair. Along the way, however, he discovers he has no artistic talent. His play is rescued and rewritten by Cheech, a hit-man gangster who comes to rehearsals as the bimbo's bodyguard, but turns out to be the artist.

Cheech works in secret, letting David take all the artistic credit. But Cheech cannot accept the compromise of having his boss' bimbo ruin what has become his play. Ironically, although he is her bodyguard, he rubs her out and is gunned down in return. The play opens to rave reviews, but David wants no part of it. Recognising that he has neither the talent nor the will of an artist, he heads back to Pittsburgh with his sweetheart.

Background: For the relationship between Helen Sinclair and David Shayne to work, David had to be much younger and more naive than Allen, so Allen cast John Cusack. After reading the script John Cusack turned up on the set and tried to impersonate Allen's speech. Allen told Cusack to stop impersonating him and act. So Cusack acted. The style of filming is very smooth - non of that hand-held camera here. The frame filled with colour and vibrancy - a stark contrast to the dull colours of *Manhattan Murder Mystery*.

Subtext: Bullets Over Broadway explores the morality of the Nietzschean artist whose will to power and will to create accept no conventional constraint or compromise. He must create his own moral universe. Cheech is the artist – his morals are different. In answer to the question at the beginning of the film, he decides to save the work – as he dies, his only concern is to improve his work. David, on the other hand, decides to save the person.

Dianne Wiest won an Oscar for her portrayal of Helen Sinclair, and she is magnificent in the role – she seduces David, completely changes his life, changes her role in the play, and controls everybody around her. She is an artist who is self-obsessed and selfish. In fact, she is the female equivalent to Cheech. Throughout the film, she puts her hand up to David's mouth and says, "Don't speak," and when Cheech dies, he tells David, "Don't speak." It is as though everybody is telling David not to write.

Like many of Allen's characters, David Shayne thinks he has integrity, compromises and then regains his integrity. Allen's characters become stronger by showing their weaknesses.

The Verdict: Some delightful playing, and costumes and set design and cinematography make this a delicious concoction to devour. However, seeing it again, and thinking about it, Allen seems to have constructed a film, like David's original play, which is full of great ideas but lacks heart. Everything is on the surface – the characters are walking around a stage created by Allen – and it has no real heart. Watch it once. 3/5

Mighty Aphrodite (1996)

Director & Writer Woody Allen

Cast: F Murray Abraham (Greek Chorus Leader), Woody Allen (Lenny), Claire Bloom (Amanda's Mother), Helena Bonham Carter (Amanda), Olympia Dukakis (Jocasta), Michael Rapaport (Kevin), Mira Sorvino (Linda Ash), David Ogden Stiers (Laius), Jack Warden (Tiresias), Peter Weller (Jerry Bender), Jeffrey Kurland (Oedipus), 95 mins

> "There are only two things that you can control in life: art and masturbation."

Story: Amanda is thinking of adopting a baby because she is too busy to give birth. Lenny is against the idea - he is worried about whose genes they would be raising. The baby could grow up to be a serial killer, or worse. They adopt a baby, Max, and Lenny is completely won over. The years pass, Max is funny and intelligent, Amanda becomes more ambitious and wants to open her own art gallery, and Lenny continues as a sports writer. As Amanda and Lenny grow apart, the idea comes into Lenny's head that if Max is so wonderful, what must Max's birth mother be like? He steals the mother's name and address, tracks her down under various aliases, finds out she has appeared in porn movies and is a prostitute. He arranges to meet her.

Linda is a tall, well-proportioned blonde, with a high-pitched voice and low IQ. She says she is always attracted to losers which is why she likes Lenny. They argue at first because Lenny becomes protective towards her, then they become friends and Lenny persuades Linda to stop selling her body. Linda's pimp objects, but Lenny pays him off with some ringside basketball tickets.

Meanwhile, Amanda is opening her own gallery, although she does not feel close enough to Lenny to inform him, and then she begins an affair with the gallery's backer, Jerry Bender.

Linda wants to meet a man who will be nice to her, someone with whom she can settle down. Lenny plays God and matches her with dumb boxer Kevin. They meet, fall for each other, then break up when he finds out Linda had been in a porn movie. As Linda and Lenny console each other (Lenny and Amanda having broken up), they kiss and make love.

Amanda decides she loves Lenny, so they get back together. Linda meets a helicopter pilot and they fall in love. She has a baby, Lenny's, but does not tell Lenny. They meet years later, admire each other's children not knowing they are the parents.

The Verdict: Although this is framed with a Greek chorus, and there are allusions to Oedipus, the death of Achilles, and other Greek figures, this is no tragedy. This is a romantic comedy with a lot of crude sexual references. Mira Sorvino as Linda gets all the best lines and deserves her Oscar. Linda appears to be like Olive in *Bullets Over Broadway*, but here she is reliving the *Pygmalion* story Allen loves so much. Lenny controls Linda's life, as Alvy controlled Annie Hall. He gives her confidence like Danny Rose gave confidence to Tina Vitale and his acts. Unfortunately, Sorvino is the only outstanding performance in a film that has ideas but lacks bite. 2/5

Everyone Says I Love You (1997)

Director & Writer Woody Allen

Cast: Alan Alda (Bob), Woody Allen (Joe), Drew Barrymore (Skylar), Lukas Haas (Scott), Goldie Hawn (Steffi), Gaby Hoffmann (Lane), Natasha Lyonne (DJ), Edward Norton (Holden), Natalie Portman (Laura), Julia Roberts (Von), Tim Roth (Charles Ferry), David Ogden Stiers (Holden's Father), 101 mins

Story: A lot of people fall into and out of love with the wrong and right people. Skylar, a romantic, leaves soft fiancée Holden for animalistic criminal sociopath Charles Ferry, and then returns to him. Von leaves actor husband Greg to be with her fantasy man Joe (who knows her deepest thoughts via Lane's eavesdropping on Von's psychoanalyst sessions), only to return to her husband. To express their internal emotions, they break into song.

Being a romantic comedy, everybody ends up okay, except the people who end up dead.

Subtext: Err. Everyone sings "I'm through with love," but they are saying, "I love you."

Background: There are many recurring themes/ideas in this: New York has rarely been so beautifully photographed; Joe goes out with the wrong type of women (nymphomaniacs, addicts, lunatics); fantasy compared with reality in Joe's relationship with Von; death and "the void" at Grandpa's funeral; Joe and ex-wife Steffi are better friends than lovers; a party where everybody is dressed as Groucho. The Groucho connection is appropriate because the Marx Brothers sang the song in *Horse Feathers* (1933). The natural way in which everybody sings and dances, and the convoluted interweaving of the characters is reminiscent of the French New Wave musicals of Jacques Demy, especially *Les Parapluies De Cherbourg* (1964) and *Les Demoiselles De Rochefort* (1967).

The Verdict: Of Allen's recent films, I find this the most disappointing. It is romantic and whimsically funny, and it has a great cast, but it feels very thin, and nothing much happens. It does, however, have one sparkling, magical moment - when Joe and Steffi dance on the bank of the River Seine in Paris. As they step and twirl, like a latter-day Fred Astaire and Ginger Rogers, Joe lets go and Steffi floats up into the air. This is worth the price of admission alone, which is why I give it... 3/5

Deconstructing Harry (1998)

Director & Writer Woody Allen

Cast: Woody Allen (Harry Block), Caroline Aaron (Doris), Kirstie Alley (Joan), Bob Balaban (Richard), Richard Benjamin (Ken), Eric Bogosian (Burt), Billy Crystal (Larry), Judy Davis (Lucy), Hazelle Goodman (Cookie), Mariel Hemingway (Beth Kramer), Amy Irving (Jane), Julie Kavner (Grace), Eric Lloyd (Hilly Block), Julia Louis-Dreyfus (Leslie), Tobey Maguire (Harvey Stern), Demi Moore (Helen), Elisabeth Shue (Fay), Stanley Tucci (Paul Epstein), Robin Williams (Mel), 95 mins

"You use sex to express every emotion except love."

Story: Harry Block, a writer of serio-comic novels, is suffering from writer's block. He is not best pleased. Neither are his ex-wives, who are upset at the way he depicts them in his novels.

Novel Extract: Ken makes love to his wife's sister, Leslie, in the house, looking out the window to make sure the rest of the family are not coming. Then, the blind grandmother enters and Ken moans in ecstasy during their conversation.

Story: Lucy, the model for Leslie, is livid and pulls a gun on Harry but misses. Harry tries to mollify Lucy by telling her his troubles and his latest short story.

Short Story: As a young man, working in a shoe shop, living with his girlfriend and writing (but using it as an excuse not to sleep with his girlfriend), he has the opportunity to sleep with an amazing Chinese hooker. He pretends he is someone else, has the greatest sex of his life and then there is a knock on the door - Death has come for him. "No, I'm only pretending - I'm really someone else." "They all say that," says Death.

Story: Harry explains to his shrink that Lucy did not shoot, which means writing saved his life. But he is suffering from writer's block. The shrink asks Harry to tell him his latest short story.

Short Story: Mel is an actor who is literally going out of focus. The cameraman says that he should have a rest to sharpen himself up. Going home, his wife Grace and the children cannot bear to look at him. When he goes to the doctor, the only solution is for Grace and the children to wear glasses.

Story: The subtext is that people have to adjust to Harry, because Harry will not adjust to the world. Harry is nervous about the honouring ceremony he is attending. He would like his son to be there, but his ex-wife, Joan, will not allow it. Joan is a shrink and that is how Harry met her.

Short Story: Paul Epstein, a writer, is undergoing therapy with Helen. He shows her some of his work, and she both admires and analyses it. It is great for Paul because Helen loves him for what he is, warts and all. But, Helen changes. She begins to find her Jewish roots, blesses the food, drink and even their lovemaking. Eventually, she falls in love with another patient, who is more in touch with Jewish traditions.

Story: Harry meets a friend, Richard, who is undergoing tests for a heart complaint. At the doctor's, Harry talks about his own problems rather than Richard's. Then Harry goes for a drink with his ex-girlfriend Fay - she is getting married to Harry's friend Larry, and they both want Harry's blessing. Fay was Eliza Dolittle to Harry's Henry Higgins. "I was in awe with you. I wasn't in love with you," Fay tells him.

Short Story: Harry wakes one morning to find the Devil has abducted his girlfriend.

Story: To satisfy his urges, Harry pays hookers to have sex with him. He tries with Cookie but he has a problem focusing. She overcomes the problem

Memoir: Harry remembers how he met Fay. He was married to Jane, and was sneaking out to a hotel to be with her neurotic sister Lucy, when he meets Fay in the elevator. Fay expressed her admiration for Harry's books,

81

Harry asked her for a drink, and they danced, made love and began living together. Harry: "You fell in love with my book, not me."

Story: Harry is off to the honouring ceremony and wants company, so he pays Cookie to accompany him. Richard comes along also. Harry kidnaps his son Hilly, so that Hilly can be proud of his father. They stop at a fair to entertain Hilly.

Memoir: Harry remembers that he argued with Jane there - she suspected that there was something going on with Lucy.

Fantasy: One of Harry's characters, his alter ego Ken, says that Harry only picks women who stop him from growing up. He then shows Harry the effect that his affair with Fay had on Jane and Lucy.

Story: Harry, with Cookie, Richard and Hilly in tow, decides to drop in on his sister Doris. She is very Jewish and the basis for Helen's conversion in his short story. Doris and her husband are still bitter about Harry's portrayal of Jewish people in his stories.

Short Story: At their *Star Wars*-themed wedding anniversary, the happily-married Dolly finds out that her husband Max may have a dark secret. Later, one of her friends tells Dolly and she confronts her husband - Max killed his wife, and two children, and his neighbour, and then ate them. The same Max who does not eat meat, and is such a fussy eater.

Memoir: Harry remembers breaking up with Joan - He had been fucking her patients.

Fantasy: Helen shows Harry that despite what she says, Doris still loves him, and defends him in front of her husband.

Story: Richard dies of a heart attack in the car. They arrive at the College and call an ambulance. Harry is falling apart, popping pills, going out of focus, and Cookie calms him down so that that he sharpens up.

Fantasy Story: Harry in an elevator going down to Hell, where he meets the Devil (Larry). Harry wants his girlfriend back.

Story: Harry is arrested for kidnapping his son, possessing Lucy's gun in his car and having drugs. Contemplating his predicament, Harry realises that he can manipulate characters, control them, but he cannot control real life. He has to make peace with his demons. Larry and Fay arrive, from their wedding, put up bail for Harry and ask for his blessing.

Fantasy: Arriving back at his apartment, Harry is ushered to an honouring ceremony - all his characters are there clapping him. Harry realises that he cannot function in life, only in art.

Story: Harry has an idea. What if he wrote a story about a writer. It is fragmented. He has a fragmented existence. Harry thinks he can use he idea as the basis of a novel. Harry is not blocked anymore.

Subtext: Part Charles Dickens' *A Christmas Carol*, part Frank Capra's *It's A Wonderful Life*, this is all Woody Allen. We see the point of view of the central character through his short stories and his memories, like in *Stardust Memories, Annie Hall* and *Another Woman.* The three types of women - dependable, neurotic, vibrant - recall other films like *Interiors* and *Hannah And Her Sisters.* The *Pygmalion* theme is also in *Annie Hall.*

A student says to Harry, "I like deconstructing your work because the characters seem sad, but underneath they're really happy." This is a continuation of Allen's theme from *Manhattan* - that modern people, who are basically happy, fill their lives with neurotic problems just so that they have something to do or feel guilty about.

Harry is one of Allen's most despicable characters. He repeatedly cheats on his wife and girlfriend, both in real life and in his fiction. He is completely self-obsessed. He has no real friends - he has to hire a hooker and kidnap his son to bring them to his honouring ceremony. And in the end, what does Harry learn? That he has to know himself. That he has to think about his life in order to write about himself again. He is perpetuating his own myth.

This is a sad film - Harry welcomes the appreciation of his characters, and his readers, and academia, but in the end you cannot see any of his friends or family applauding.

Visual Ideas: This film is edited in an arresting manner. It begins with Lucy getting out of a yellow cab, very angry. The time is cut up and rearranged, over and over, in every permutation you can imagine.

The Verdict: A real return to form for Allen after a couple of so-so movies. This film has bite. It is so good, I was toying with the idea of calling this book *Deconstructing Woody.* It was either that or *Woody Interiors.* Be thankful I did not use either. 4/5

Celebrity (1999)

Director & Writer Woody Allen

Cast: Hank Azaria (David), Kenneth Branagh (Lee Simon), Judy Davis (Robin Simon), Leonardo DiCaprio (Brandon Darrow), Melanie Griffith (Nicole Oliver), Famke Janssen (Bonnie), Michael Lerner (Dr Lupus), Joe Mantegna (Tony Gardella), Bebe Neuwirth (Hooker), Winona Ryder (Nola), Charlize Theron (Supermodel), Patti D'Arbanville (Iris), Gretchen Mol, Donald Trump, Mary Jo Buttafuoco, Joey Buttafuoco, Bruce Jay Friedman (Elaine's Book Party Guest), Alfred Molina, Vanessa Redgrave, 113 mins

Story: Lee Simon is a journalist who has broken up with his wife Robin. He spends a lot of time writing articles on movie stars and models, and tries to get into bed with them figuratively (trying to sell his story idea) and literally. The problem is that he is totally at odds with this world because he wants to write a novel that has integrity - he does not see this media world as having integrity.

Robin is devastated by her break-up with Lee. She feels her life has been torn apart. When she meets Tony Gardella, she finds he is a real person with a family around him. Tony gives Robin a job in TV, and somehow she ends up with her own TV show, and becomes famous.

Lee writes his novel, and then cheats on his girlfriend, who throws the only copy of the manuscript into the Hudson River. At the end, Lee sits entranced at the cinema screen, still dreaming.

Subtext: Lee's novel is a symbol of his integrity. When he cheats on his girlfriend, it is appropriate that he loses his novel. The loss of the manuscript echoes *Husbands And Wives*. The final shot of Lee looking at the screen - the healing power of fantasy - is reminiscent of Cecilia at the end of *The Purple Rose Of Cairo*. The fickle finger of fame - who knows where it will strike next?

The Verdict: Kenneth Branagh does an impression of Woody Allen which is both entertaining and vaguely annoying at the same time. Judy Davis is superb, as always, and Joe Mantegna exudes integrity. This is fun from beginning to end, and has an appropriate bittersweet love-hate relationship with fame and celebrity, but it feels very like Allen is regurgitating old material. 3/5

Sweet And Lowdown (1999)

Director & Writer Woody Allen

Cast: Sean Penn (Emmet Ray), Samantha Morton (Hattie), Uma Thurman (Blanche), Anthony LaPlagia (Al Torrio), Gretchen Mol (Ellie), John Waters (Mr Haynes), Woody Allen, Nat Hentoff, Douglas McGrath, 95 mins

Story: In the Jazz Age of the 1930s, one guitarist rules supreme - the gypsy Django Reinhardt. Luckily he's in Europe, so the best player on the American continent is Emmet Ray. Woody Allen, Nat Hentoff and other jazz historians and aficionados tell the tale of the elusive Emmet Ray in a mockumentary that evokes *Zelig*, *Broadway Danny Rose* and *Take The Money And Run*.

Emmet Ray is a pimp (he prefers the term 'manager') who complains of a low take from the girls. "Business is slow - it's a Jewish holiday," they tell him. Playing pool for money and losing, drinking lots of alcohol, a klepto-maniac, Emmet climbs onto stage and plays a real sweet guitar. He is transformed from boar to genius. One of his dreams is to build a giant crescent moon and to make his entrance sitting on it as it descends onto the stage. He spends his own money to get the moon made but, afraid he might fall, he drinks himself stiff beforehand. Consequently, he is too drunk to sit still and falls from the moon. Afterwards, as he burns the moon, he says, "Sooner or later, everybody's dreams go up in smoke."

Emmet's idea of a good time is going to the dump to shoot rats, or watching trains. He is happy to share his enthusiasms with his women friends. Disappointed that he is so distant when making love, one of the women says that they want more emotion from him. "I let my feelings out in my music," Emmet tells her.

Whilst working at a hotel, Emmet picks up Hattie, a mute. Annoyed that she is not witty and fun, he treats her rotten, calling her dumb and a halfwit. He is surprised when, at his hotel room, she comes on to him all of a sudden, tearing off his clothes. After they make love, Emmet plays his guitar, and it is at that moment, expressing his love, that she falls for him. They are together and when Emmet decides it is time to leave for a gig in Hollywood, Hattie goes along. "I'm an artist, a truly great artist," he tells her, and explains that being sweet, like her, "won't get you anywhere in life." Of course, Emmet appears in a background band of a movie and Hattie is spotted by a film director and is cast in some movies. They return to New York.

Some time later, the story is picked up. Emmet meets debutante-turned-writer Blanche Williams, who is excited by the disparity between Emmet's outward lowdown crudeness and the beautiful music inside him. She constantly interviews and analyses him, writing in her book that he has 'the ego of a genius... I must get used to it.' They marry, but they are not suited and Blanche goes off with a Mafia bodyguard, excited by the danger surrounding him and no doubt planning another book.

Emmet visits Hattie and asks her to come back with him but she is married. Upset, he goes to watch the trains and plays the music he played to her. He stops, takes the guitar which he has loved and protected more than anything else, and smashes it to pieces.

Woody Allen says that Emmet's last few records, around this time, were the best, the sweetest he'd ever done. Emmet had become as good as, if not better than, Django Reinhardt, because he allowed himself to feel.

Subtext: Emmet is a complex character full of contradictions. His actions and words are horrible. Blanche says to him one time: "Not only are you vain and egotistical, but you're crude as well." The crux of the matter is that he considers himself a true artist, and he loves his art more than the women he beds. He only expresses his true emotions through his music. The irony, of course, is that this is exactly the reason he is not the best guitar player in the world. This concern with the artist and his art is a constant theme in

Allen's films, the most recent examples being *Celebrity*, *Deconstructing Harry* and *Bullets Over Broadway*.

Hattie echoes Emmet because she cannot express her love for Emmet through words. However, she does show her love by her actions. She stays with him. She remembers his birthday and gives him a pair of gloves because she wants to protect his hands - his hands play music for her, and they are the way Emmet shows his love for her. (He is ruled by his head. She is ruled by her heart. He is lowdown. She is sweet.)

There are recurring Allen themes. Emmet wants fame, but it is handed on a platter to Hattie in Hollywood, which is similar to the way it happens in *Celebrity*. There is a *Pygmalion* scene, where Emmet buys clothes for Hattie, but she continues to wear her old hat! Emmet will not commit to a relationship - a problem with most of Allen's male characters.

Background: This film marks Allen's first collaboration with cinematographer Zhao Fei, who worked on *Raise The Red Lantern* (1991) and other sumptuous Zhang Yimou movies. Unable to speak English, Allen and Fei communicated via a team of translators – ironic considering the communication problems of the central characters. Music arranger and conductor Dick Hyman, a constant Allen collaborator, suggested virtuoso jazz guitarist Howard Alden to play Emmet's 30 solos. They are superb, and Sean Penn learnt how to play the guitar so that he could mime authentically.

The Verdict: This is a delightful movie, full of little surprises. Both Penn and Morton are wonderful in difficult roles. Penn manages the trick of being unlikeable but understandable. Morton manages to convey her emotions through body language - Allen rarely gives her close-ups to make her life easier. The period detail, as always, is beautifully rendered and the storytelling is faultless. On top of that it has some magic music which brings you to a different place. 4/5

Small Time Crooks (2000)

Director & Writer Woody Allen

Cast: Woody Allen (Ray Winkler), Tracey Ullman (Frenchy Winkler), Elaine May (May), Hugh Grant (David), Michael Rapaport (Denny), Jon Lovitz (Benny), Elaine Stritch (Chi Chi Potter), 95 mins

Story: Ray Winkler is a small-time crook, who was nicknamed 'The Brain' in jail, only he's too dumb to realise the other cons were ribbing him. The Brain has promised to go straight, but he has a brilliant idea - buy a place a couple of doors down from the bank, set up a business there, and tunnel in through the basement - only he needs wife Frenchy's savings to set it up. Heading a team of dumb and dumber crooks, they start drilling, with

Frenchy selling her homemade cookies as a front. The drilling is a bust, but Frenchy hits paydirt with the cookies - they make lots of dough.

Fastforward to their new corporation, Sunset Farms, which franchises out the cookie stores. They make great flavours like Chicken Chip and Tuna Mint. Frenchy decides that she will use the money to improve herself and hires David to teach her how to appreciate the arts. This, she thinks, will allow her to enter high society, but all this society wants from her is financial donations - they are the unmentioned big-time crooks. Ray does not agree with these changes so the couple splits up.

Ray spends his time with May, Frenchy's dumb cousin who is strangely affecting, and he decides to steal a diamond necklace - to avoid suspicion, Ray replaces it with a replica. When Frenchy gets back from Venice she finds out that the accountants have stolen all the money. Without any money (Ray messed up and kept the replica necklace) the couple get back together.

Subtext: Allen is showing different levels of society and their interaction. When Frenchy and Ray are among thieves, there is friendship and trust. When they are among the rich, the rich are only there to get money out of the Winklers. Even the police and the accountants are out to steal their (legitimate) money. Ray is not doing the stealing (his 'art') for the money. Ray likes stealing, and practising that, even if he is not particularly proficient at it. He wants a beer and a cheeseburger rather than a fancy meal. He is not interested in social climbing either: "My idea of fun is not opera and ruins. I get enough sleep at home."

Frenchy, a former exotic dancer, tries to transform her appearance (wearing tasteless clothes and decorating her apartment in a vulgar manner, an extension of her kitsch sensibilities) and her mind (she hires David to teach her about the finer things in life). This is the *Pygmalion* story again.

Throughout the movie, there are revealing references: the opera *La Traviata* is about a man in love with a loose woman whom society rejects; the Brit Duke of Windsor married the socially unacceptable Yank divorcee Mrs Simpson; Ray and May watch *White Heat*, the bit where James Cagney wants to be 'top of the world'; *The Treasure Of The Sierra Madre* (misquoted here on purpose as "The Treasure Of Treasure Island") is about people who do anything to get money only for it to be blown away as dust in the wind (just as the false diamonds are reduced to dust at the end); Ray mistaking bandleader Harry James for novelist Henry James (Henry often wrote about gullible Americans being misled by sophisticated and duplicitous Europeans).

In the end, when they strip away all the money and clothes, Ray and Frenchy come to realise that they only need each other.

Background: Small Time Crooks was distributed in the US by Dream-Works SKG, and marketed as a comedy rather than as a Woody Allen picture. It returned the biggest gross ever on a Woody Allen film, and has resulted in a three-picture deal with DreamWorks SKG.

The Verdict: This enjoyable light comedy has many nice moments of slapstick and dialogue. (Ray: "I've got a lot of things on my mind." Frenchy: "Your mind don't hold a lot.") It works because of strong performances from Tracey Ullman and, especially, Elaine May. Amazingly, Allen finds space for some subtext as well, but it is hardly new or profound. 3/5

The Curse Of The Jade Scorpion (2001)

Director & Writer: Woody Allen

Cast: Woody Allen, Dan Aykroyd, Elizabeth Berkley, Helen Hunt, Wallace Shawn, David Ogden Stiers, Charlize Theron

Story: Set in the 1940s, this romantic comedy is about a jewel heist investigated by insurance man Allen, whose office (run by Dan Aykroyd) is being updated by Helen Hunt to use modern methods.

Background: The production ran from September 25 to early December 2000 in New York City. Release date in America is August 10, 2001.

The Last Laugh

"Dying is hard. Comedy is easy."

What does Allen do now? When his personal life became public gossip, he produced Allen-lite material - enjoyable pastiches of Alfred Hitchcock thrillers or Vincente Minnelli musicals or Preston Sturges screwball comedies. Serious elements have been included in the scripts, but they have not been allowed to take over the style of the movie.

In recent years, Allen has appeared as an actor on TV and in movies. In 1994, he directed and starred in a TV version of his play *Don't Drink The Water*, then the following year he acted in a TV version of Neil Simon's play *The Sunshine Boys* with Peter Falk. His film acting has consisted of Godard's *King Lear* (1987), Paul Mazursky's *Scenes From A Mall* (1991), *Antz* (1998) and a few others.

Deconstructing Harry and *Sweet And Lowdown* indicate that Allen has not lost his touch, and still has vital things to say. However, his muse has currently been tickling his funny bone and Allen promises a couple more comedies before returning to a more sombre tone. Whatever the topic, I suspect Allen will continue to surprise and confound his admirers in future films.

"Chapter One: He was as tough and romantic as the city he loved. Behind his black-rimmed glasses was the coiled sexual power of a jungle cat.... New York was his town. And it always would be."

Reference Materials

Books

Brooklyn Is Not Expanding: Woody Allen's Comic Universe by Annette Wernblad, Associated University Presses, US, 1992

...But We Need The Eggs: The Magic Of Woody Allen by Diane Jacobs, St Martin's Press, US, 1982

Everything You Always Wanted To Know About Woody Allen by Frank Weimann, Shapolsky Publishers, US, 1991

The Films Of Woody Allen by Sam B Girgus, Cambridge University Press, UK, 1993

I Dream Of Woody by Dee Burton, William Morrow, US, 1984

The Illustrated Woody Allen Reader by Linda Sunshine, Knopf, US, 1993

Loser Take All: The Comic Art Of Woody Allen by Maurice Yacowar, Continuum, US, 1991. This is a great book for anybody who wants to find out about the subtext of Woody's work. Yacowar has put a lot of thought into this and, although the later, updated, section perhaps seems a bit thinner than the text from the earlier edition, (and it sometimes reads as though he is forcing the films to fit a preconceived formula) this is informative and engrossing.

Love, Sex, Death, And The Meaning Of Life: Woody Allen's Comedy by Foster Hirsch, McGraw-Hill, US, 1981

Woody Allen by Nancy Pogel, Twayne, US, 1987

Woody Allen, A Biography by Lee Guthrie, Drake Publishers, US, 1978

Woody Allen, A Biography by Eric Lax, Jonathan Cape, UK, 1991. This is probably the best Woody Allen biography we are going to get. I say this because Lax is a friend of Allen's and has been for some time. Lax is relaxed, anecdotal and has access to all Allen's collaborators. He also has a keen analytical eye concerning both the films and Allen. I would heartily recommend you to go out and buy a copy of this.

Woody Allen's Angst: Philosophical Commentaries On His Serious Films by Sander H Lee, McFarland & Company, US, 1997

Woody Allen An Illustrated Biography by Miles Palmer, Proteus, US, 1980. Try to avoid this one at all costs. It has big type printed on big pages. It is a collection of bits of dialogue and stories from the films and Allen's stage work. When they run out of big photos to fit on their big pages, they draw big pictures to fill in the spaces. Not good.

Woody Allen At Work: The Photographs Of Brian Hamill edited by Diana Murphy, Harry M Abrams, US, 1995

The Woody Allen Companion by Stephen J Spignesi, Andrews And McMeel, US, 1992

Woody Allen: His Films And Career by Douglas Brode, Citadel Press, US, 1985

Woody Allen: Joking Aside by Gerald McKnight, W H Allen, UK, 1983

Woody Allen: New Yorker by Graham McCann, Basil Blackwell, US, 1990

Woody Allen On Location by Thierry de Navacelle, Morrow, US, 1987. In many ways this could have been a great book about the making of *Radio Days* but, Navacelle is so overawed by Allen, he constantly pulls back, afraid of offending the great director. Still, let us be fair, the background detail is enormous - for every day of filming Navacelle lists which scenes are shot, how many seconds and minutes of screen time were filmed, how many takes and how many prints of that take, who was present on set, the difficulties encountered, the bets and gambling on set, the liaisons, what Woody did, and so on. At the end of the book, there is a full script, which includes all the scenes cut from the final version, and those scenes not shot. A comprehensive record, but it is hard work piling through all the details.

Woody Allen On Woody Allen: In Conversation With Stig Björkman, Faber & Faber, 1994. Initially, I was very excited by this book because I thought it would reveal quite a lot about Allen – as though it was some kind of Rossetta stone. However, it turns out to be repetitive, and Allen is reticent to tell us anything more than what has already been printed. Having said that, there is much to recommend it, and you get to learn about Allen through osmosis rather than through any explicit statements.

Woody Allen: Profane And Sacred by Richard Aloysius Blake, Scarecrow Press, US, 1995

Woody Allen: The Crown Prince Of American Humor by Bill Adler & J Feinman, Pinnacle, US, 1975

Woody And His Women by Tim Carroll, Little,Brown, US/UK, 1993. A hack and slash biography concentrating on the more sensationalistic and prurient aspects of Woody's life. Obviously compiled from various thin sources and padded out with background detail.

The Internet

http://www.geocities.com/SunsetStrip/Club/9542/woody.html - A most excellent site which features long reviews of virtually every film, plus links and photos. Go here first.

http://www.media.uio.no/studentene/ragnhild.paalsrud/woody/Woody.html - A guide to Woody Allen his films, his books, his life, although now about 5 years out of date.

http://www.geocities.com/~madcap/Woody/index.html - Very useful Frequently Asked Questions site. It even tells you the name of the font Woody uses on his credit sequences (known as both Windsor and Clearface).

http://www.flf.com/harry/index.html - Official Site for *Deconstructing Harry*.

http://www.spe.sony.com/classics/sweetandlowdown/index.html - Official site for *Sweet And Lowdown*. Includes a lot of interesting background information.

http://www.amazon.com/smalltimecrooks - Official site for *Small Time Crooks*. Includes an interview with Woody.

http://www.dreamworks.com/jadescorpion/ - Official site for *The Curse Of The Jade Scorpion*.

Usenet groups: news:alt.fan.woody-allen, news:alt.sex.woody-allen

To subscribe to the Woody Allen mailing list, send the following message to listserver@westga.edu: subscribe WOODY-L First name Last name

The Essential Library

Build up your library with new titles every month

Alfred Hitchcock by Paul Duncan

More than 20 years after his death, Alfred Hithcock is still a household name, most people in the Western world have seen at least one of his films, and he popularised the action movie format we see every week on the cinema screen. He was both a great artist and dynamite at the box office. This book examines the genius and enduring popularity of one of the most influential figures in the history of the cinema!

Stanley Kubrick by Paul Duncan

Kubrick's work, like all masterpieces, has a timeless quality. His vision is so complete, the detail so meticulous, that you believe you are in a three-dimensional space displayed on a two-dimensional screen. He was commercially successful because he embraced traditional genres like War (*Paths Of Glory*, *Full Metal Jacket*), Crime (*The Killing*), Science Fiction (*2001*), Horror (*The Shining*) and Love (*Barry Lyndon*). At the same time, he stretched the boundaries of film with controversial themes: underage sex (*Lolita*); ultra violence (*A Clockwork Orange*); and erotica (*Eyes Wide Shut*).

Orson Welles by Martin Fitzgerald

The popular myth is that after the artistic success of *Citizen Kane* it all went downhill from there for Orson Welles, that he was some kind of fallen genius. Yet, despite overwhelming odds, he went on to make great Films Noirs like *The Lady From Shanghai* and *Touch Of Evil*. He translated Shakespeare's work into films with heart and soul (*Othello*, *Chimes At Midnight*, *Macbeth*), and he refused to take the bite out of modern literature, giving voice to bitterness, regret and desperation in *The Magnificent Ambersons* and *The Trial*. Far from being down and out, Welles became one of the first cutting-edge independent filmmakers.

Film Noir by Paul Duncan

The laconic private eye, the corrupt cop, the heist that goes wrong, the femme fatale with the rich husband and the dim lover - these are the trademark characters of Film Noir. This book charts the progression of the Noir style as a vehicle for film-makers who wanted to record the darkness at the heart of American society as it emerged from World War to the Cold War. As well as an introduction explaining the origins of Film Noir, seven films are examined in detail and an exhaustive list of over 500 Films Noirs are listed.

The Essential Library

Build up your library with new titles every month

Film Directors:

Jane Campion (£2.99)
Jackie Chan (£2.99)
David Cronenberg (£3.99)
Alfred Hitchcock (£3.99)
Stanley Kubrick (£2.99)
David Lynch (£3.99)
Sam Peckinpah (£2.99)
Orson Welles (£2.99)
Steven Spielberg (£3.99)

John Carpenter (£3.99)
Joel & Ethan Coen (£3.99)
Terry Gilliam (£2.99)
Krzysztof Kieslowski (£2.99)
Sergio Leone (£3.99)
Brian De Palma (£2.99)
Ridley Scott (£3.99)
Billy Wilder (£3.99)

Film Genres:

Film Noir (£3.99)
Horror Films (£3.99)
Spaghetti Westerns (£3.99)
Blaxploitation Films (£3.99)

Hong Kong Heroic Bloodshed (£2.99)
Slasher Movies (£3.99)
Vampire Films (£2.99)

Film Subjects:

Laurel & Hardy (£3.99)
Steve McQueen (£2.99)
The Oscars® (£3.99)
Bruce Lee (£3.99)

Marx Brothers (£3.99)
Marilyn Monroe (£3.99)
Filming On A Microbudget (£3.99)

TV:

Doctor Who (£3.99)

Literature:

Cyberpunk (£3.99)
Hitchhiker's Guide (£3.99)
Terry Pratchett (£3.99)

Philip K Dick (£3.99)
Noir Fiction (£2.99)
Sherlock Holmes (£3.99)

Ideas:

Conspiracy Theories (£3.99)
Feminism (£3.99)

Nietzsche (£3.99)

History:

Alchemy & Alchemists (£3.99)

The Crusades (£3.99)

Available at all good bookstores, or send a cheque to: **Pocket Essentials (Dept WA2), 18 Coleswood Rd, Harpenden, Herts, AL5 1EQ, UK**. Please make cheques payable to 'Oldcastle Books.' Add 50p postage & packing for each book in the UK and £1 elsewhere.

US customers can send $6.95 plus $1.95 postage & packing for each book to: **Trafalgar Square Publishing, PO Box 257, Howe Hill Road, North Pomfret, Vermont 05053, USA**. e-mail: tsquare@sover.net

Customers worldwide can order online at **www.pocketessentials.com**.

The Essential Library

Build up your library with new titles every month

Tim Burton by Colin Odell & Michelle Le Blanc, £3.99

Tim Burton makes films about outsiders on the periphery of society. His heroes are psychologically scarred, perpetually naive and childlike, misunderstood or unintentionally disruptive. They upset convential society and morality. Even his villains are rarely without merit - circumstance blurs the divide between moral fortitude and personal action. But most of all, his films have an aura of the fairytale, the fantastical and the magical.

Film Music by Paul Tonks, £3.99

From *Ben-Hur* to *Star Wars* and *Psycho* to *Scream*, film music has played an essential role in such genre-defining classics. Making us laugh, cry, and jump with fright, it's the manipulative tool directors cannot do without. The turbulent history, the ever-changing craft, the reclusive or limelight-loving superstars, the enthusiastic world of fandom surrounding it, and the best way to build a collection, is all streamlined into a user-friendly guide for buffs and novices alike.

Woody Allen (Revised & Updated Edition) by Martin Fitzgerald, £3.99

Woody Allen: Neurotic. Jewish. Funny. Inept. Loser. A man with problems. Or so you would think from the characters he plays in his movies. But hold on. Allen has written and directed 30 films. He may be a funny man, but he is also one of the most serious American film-makers of his generation. This revised and updated edition includes *Sweet And Lowdown* and *Small Time Crooks*.

American Civil War by Phil Davies, £3.99

The American Civil War, fought between North and South in the years 1861-1865, was the bloodiest and most traumatic war in American history. Rival visions of the future of the United States faced one another across the battlefields and, as in any civil war, families and friends were bitterly divided by the conflict. Phil Davies looks at the deep-rooted causes of the war, so much more complicated than the simple issue of slavery.

American Indian Wars by Howard Hughes, £3.99

At the beginning of the 1840s the proud tribes of the North American Indians looked across the plains at the seemingly unstoppable expansion of the white man's West. During the decades of conflict that followed, as the new world pushed onward, the Indians saw their way of life disappear before their eyes. Over the next 40 years they clung to a dream of freedom and a continuation of their traditions, a dream that was repeatedly shattered by the whites.

0362 96